MW00622571

# Celebrating the
# Graying Church

# Celebrating the Graying Church

## Mutual Ministry Today, Legacies Tomorrow

Richard P. Olson

An Alban Institute Book

ROWMAN & LITTLEFIELD
*Lanham • Boulder • New York • London*

Published by Rowman & Littlefield
An imprint of The Rowman & Littlefield Publishing Group, Inc.
4501 Forbes Boulevard, Suite 200, Lanham, Maryland 20706
www.rowman.com

6 Tinworth Street, London SE11 5AL, United Kingdom

Copyright © 2020 by The Rowman & Littlefield Publishing Group, Inc.

*All rights reserved.* No part of this book may be reproduced in any form or by any electronic or mechanical means, including information storage and retrieval systems, without written permission from the publisher, except by a reviewer who may quote passages in a review.

British Library Cataloguing in Publication Information Available

**Library of Congress Cataloging-in-Publication Data Available**

ISBN 978-1-5381-3966-0 (cloth : alk. paper)
ISBN 978-1-5381-3967-7 (pbk. : alk. paper)
ISBN 978-1-5381-3968-4 (electronic)

♾™ The paper used in this publication meets the minimum requirements of American National Standard for Information Sciences—Permanence of Paper for Printed Library Materials, ANSI/NISO Z39.48-1992.

# Contents

# Acknowledgments

I am grateful to many persons who helped and contributed to this journey.

Thank you to the colleagues who are doing ministry with older adults and who agreed to an interview with me. I quoted some of you. All of your wisdom added depth to what I am saying.

Also, thanks to the churches whose stories I tell.

I am appreciative of my editors at Rowman & Littlefield. Thanks to Rolf Janke for coaching me to a proposal that addressed a felt need and was accepted. Thanks to Natalie Mandziuk and her colleagues for making the manuscript better and guiding it on to completion.

I am grateful to Jon Dedon, M.D., for enriching the conversations on location, housing, illness, and treatment out of his wisdom and experience as a Geriatrician. Thanks to Cynthia (Cindy) Haynes for sharing reflections on being a parish nurse and on relocation.

I hope that I have honored the older generations in Mary Ann's and my family. They have loved, guided, and mentored us. Now that we are the oldest surviving generation, we appreciate even more their wisdom and kindness. A similar appreciation goes to the older adults in the churches I served over the years and to the students of all ages (some of them seniors) who engaged these topics with me at Central Baptist Theological Seminary.

Thanks to the staff of Oakwood Village, Prairie Ridge in Madison, Wisconsin, our home for the last three years. I formally interviewed three staff members. With several others, neither they nor I knew I was interviewing them, but information and perspective from those conversations came to me as I wrote.

And thanks to my fellow residents. In this community, I have shared life with a larger population of older adults than ever before. I have come to enjoy and admire many of you. A number of you have given me permission to tell something of your story, and for that I am grateful.

In response to these gifts, may this book enrich and empower those who minister with older adults as well as these fascinating elders themselves.

# Introduction

## *Consider a Different Perspective on the Graying Church*

Listen to me, O house of Jacob . . . even to your old age I am [God], even when you turn away I will carry you. I have made, and I will bear; I will carry and will save.

—Isaiah 46:3a,4.

I will always remember Violet McCaw with appreciation and love. She was my wife Mary Ann's grandmother, and for a number of years after her husband died, she would come and live with us a few months each year. Soon after she arrived, she would bake cinnamon rolls that were a delight from the first scent of baking bread down to the last morsel. And her pies! She made pie crusts that were a treat in themselves. Each time she came, she would bake each family member's favorite pie (and that person got the extra piece).

She would gently prune the African Violets, and, in a few days, they would start blossoming again. Certain soap opera "stories" were a favorite time of her day, her hands always busy as she watched. She would quickly crochet an afghan for us whenever we could afford the yarn.

She slept in the same room as our youngest daughter, Laurie, then a toddler, and they greatly enjoyed being roommates, particularly their going to sleep and waking up conversations. At a time when Mary Ann and I, despite our best intentions, might not have had all the time our three daughters needed, grandma would be there when they got home from school. She would greet them, possibly with a snack, perhaps to hear their experiences, quite probably to play a game of Canasta or two. Though she had very little formal education, she brought a wealth of crafts, skills, family wisdom, and care into our lives. After a few months, the pull of home and friends would get stronger, and we would reluctantly bid her farewell till the next year.

1

I did not recognize it at the time, but living with us Grandma McCaw had one more gift—she showed us how to grow old.

As I remember her fondly, I still have a nagging question of myself. Would I have discovered how special she was and how many gifts she had if I had been her pastor rather than her grandson-in-law? How might we have experienced each other in one of the churches I served in my forty years of parish ministry? I am afraid my answer is "Maybe, maybe not."

In those years, I tried to provide good pastoral care to older adults and to give at least some support to the groups and organizations they had created. But the more intentional focus—both of those churches and me—was young families, children, and youths. For, we believed, that is how a church could be strong, its future assured.

There was a problem with that approach then, and it is an even greater problem now. Presently, a growing portion of those who remain within our churches, agencies, and other ministries are older adults. Of course, new approaches, effort, and creativity are also needed in engaging today's younger populations.

At the same time, I call us to celebrate the graying church. Be enriched in discovering the history, interests, and gifts of elders. Claim and engage their (our) passion and desire to leave a worthy legacy of our faith, lives, and commitments. There is a new "age of aging" going on, larger, stronger, more enduring than the past. Ministry with this new generation of older adults is an opportunity, a need, and a challenge.

In writing this, I have been struggling with my pronouns. On one hand, I speak as a fellow professional church leader to my colleagues in various ministries. I am a parish minister with many years of experience, a pastoral counselor, and a professor of pastoral theology who, among other topics, offered courses on life stages. (I almost wrote, I *was* a minister. However, though retired, no one has fired me or withdrawn my credentials.)

At the same time, I speak from within the older adult population. Now in our eighties, my wife Mary Ann and I moved to a new city to be near children and grandchildren. We bought into and live in a thriving older adult community.

There is a social science research method called "participant observation." As the title implies, the social scientist enters the life of a group, a tribe, a community. As much as possible, the researcher participates fully and completely into that group under consideration. But this person also is an investigator from outside, trying to understand the explored community better. While I did not intentionally plan it, I seem to have become a participant observer in a retirement community and in the population of older adults. As I visit with people at meals or the activities and outings offered here, I learn more and become more deeply involved in this age group.

I have also interviewed more than a dozen religious leaders who minister with older adults, talked with staff persons in this retirement community, engaged several discussion groups with older adults, and read widely. I am excited to carry on a conversation with these varied resources and share discoveries about ministry possibilities in this new age of elderhood.

For the first few months here, I found it strange to live among so many people using walkers or in wheelchairs (motorized or manual) or struggling with sight or hearing issues. As I have lived here longer, I now see that those handicaps and aids are secondary characteristics. More and more, I see persons' primary characteristics. I experience how alive, creative, and thriving we elders are. We do not let these difficulties—or a chronic disease or two—keep us from a full life. To give a few examples, we grow gardens and share our produce with each other, edit and circulate a monthly newspaper, run a small grocery store, manage a little library, do small "handyman" service projects, provide lay leadership in the chapel services, create numerous game, learning and service groups, and so much more. And we provide friendship and support to each other in many ways. There are gifts here that would enrich any community open to welcoming and receiving these older adults. We elders also have our needs and are grateful when a church or other agency is sensitive to them.

I am aware that the members of my retirement community are but one part of the older population—we are mostly Euro-Americans and have enough income to pay the initial "life deposit" and the monthly fees to live here. However, I will be aware of others as I write. And so, I will speak both from within my profession and within my life stage—sometimes in the same sentence! I advocate celebration of the graying church and moving more deeply into mutual ministry for, with, and by older adults. Here is the journey I propose in this book.

We begin by looking afresh at the change in aging population in chapter 1. Then in chapter 2, we explore some of the barriers that need to be overcome for effective ministry to happen. In the third chapter, we look at a number of elders with new eyes to see their gifts and hear their stories. In chapter 4, I take you within the playfulness, humor, and laughter that abound at times among elders.

The years also bring diminishment of strength, grief, and, probably, some of the chronic illnesses common among the aging. This in turn means that decisions must be faced about what needs to change and where to live—the topic of the fifth and sixth chapters. As powers decrease and some roles diminish a question elders ask is, "Why am I here?" Frail older adults may ask an even more urgent question, "Why am I *still* here?" We discuss these searches in chapter 7.

Another form of this life quest for elders is the question "What do I want my legacy to be?" or, similarly, "How can my passions and commitments be sustained beyond my life?" This is the topic of chapter 8. In chapter 9, we note that the journeys of aging impel many into spiritual searching, and, quite possibly, spiritual growth. Lest this seem too philosophical and remote, there are countless "hands on" and advocacy activities that make life richer. And these can be offered to senior adults, or by them—the subject of chapter 10.

The end of the older adult life stage is dying and death. This calls for reflection and attention to one's relationships. Elders may also want to discuss and give direction about what treatments they want or do not want when they are in the last stages of life—the subject of chapter 11. Further, they may have directions, guidance, or requests for after they have died. This may include worship experiences, stewardship of their bodies, memorials, bequests, and grief support for the survivors—the subject of chapter 12.

Ministry with us elders has many joys and many sorrows. Thoughtful and sensitive church and religious leaders can enrich these lives so much and be equally enriched in the ministering. The story of four churches that found ways to do this well and a few thoughts on how to get there are the subjects of chapter 13.

At the end of each chapter, there will be a list of topics and questions. These can be used in a variety of ways—for one's own personal reflection, or for a conversation with one or more professional colleagues interested in this topic. The questions might also be useful for interviewing of older adults, or for leading a conversation and support group of older adults.

I believe in the revelatory power of stories. And so, these pages will include many stories. These will be both from my experience and from what I have heard or read.

Religious leaders will find themselves in a wide variety of circumstances in all this. There are hospital, hospice, and retirement community chaplains. Some may be serving a shrinking, dying(?), church, and others may serve a vigorous, though aging community. Some may be looking for a new way of expressing care in their communities. There are churches in communities where many elders are leaving and others where many elders are arriving.

My hope is that at very least, this book will stir mutually enriching conversations between elders and their religious leaders and caregivers. I also hope that some may see elders with new eyes and relate to them in new ways. That will be very special, for as much as we olders like and enjoy our contemporaries, a relationship with a younger person is a lovely gift and delight. It may be that exploring these questions with the elders near you, an exciting new paradigm of ministry will emerge. May there be many gifts giving and receiving in your ministries.

One more topic, as we begin. That is the question about terminology. What words should be used about us? We have been called seniors, senior citizens, older adults, and worse. Some speak of us as elders. However, for some, the term "elder" denotes a position of wisdom and respect for accumulated knowledge and perspective. Observers have noted that while there are more older people, there are fewer elders, or fewer seen in that role, whether they qualify or not.

One person has suggested a new term for us—"olders." And still another has suggested "perennials." Another speaks of "seasoned adults." Since I will be speaking a lot about this population, I will use a mixture of those terms, except for perennial that reminds me more of gardens than people. I will probably use the term "elders" as both a general description and a designation of a certain role in society.

Another question about terminology is how people should be addressed. Some older adults resent a person one-fourth their age calling them by their first name. I understand that but don't mind, myself. It seems friendly to me. What about when a younger woman calls an old man like me "honey" or "sweetie"? I chuckle at the playfulness and kindness. Others do not agree.

I must admit, that when entering a retirement community, I lost almost all of my professional identity. I had been Dr. Olson, a respected pastoral educator. No one speaks to me that way nor asks for the leadership gifts I offered in that profession. I miss it—and so I sit at a computer, attempting to create something out of that identity.

There is another vocabulary question—what about gender language when speaking theologically or quoting a Bible passage? I aspire to inclusive language on that front, but once in a while, it just doesn't work in a given passage for me. I have to plead a bit of inconsistency on that topic.

One other topic of perspective—I submitted a proposal, signed a contract, and wrote much of what follows long before I had ever heard of COVID-19 and barely knew what a pandemic was. I have annotated, edited, and polished this manuscript while our retirement community insists we refrain from social activities and stay isolated from each other. I offer this anticipating a post-pandemic world. I will speak of the pandemic but briefly, noting where things we experienced and learned might have carry over value to our life after it is over. At the end of this book, I will offer a brief postscript chapter on ministry with older adults after the pandemic.

So, thanks for listening and welcome to our further conversations. I have discovered some things that may enrich your ministry and your life, and I am eager to share them with you.

## FOR REFLECTING AND EXPLORING

1. Interview one or more of the longest-term members in your church (or other ministry) and invite them to tell their story. Why did you join this church (or organization)? What drew you to it? What are some of your greatest memories of it? What experiences within it do you treasure?

How is the church doing with you in the present? What do you wish the leaders of the church knew about you and your contemporaries?

2. Visit an event or two where elders gather—in your church or in the wider community. What draws them there? What customs or rituals seem familiar to them, but not to you?

3. At the end of the chapter, I wrote about terms for older adults in general, and how to speak to individuals. Informed by that paragraph, ask older people how they want to be described and how they want to be addressed.

4. Visit the AARP—American Association of Retired People website or browse one of their magazines. What interests do they touch? What interest or needs do they seem to ignore?

5. Listen to your heart, take your pulse—how do you feel about getting to know elders better and exploring new avenues of mutual ministry?

## Chapter 1

# Learn about the Changing Scenes, Size, and Cohorts of Today's Elders

No more shall there be in it an infant that lives but a few days,
or an old person who does not live out a lifetime;
for one who dies at a hundred years will be considered a youth,
and one who falls short of a hundred will be considered accursed.

—Isaiah 65:20

Ten thousand people turned sixty-five today, and yesterday, and tomorrow. They enter the largest older adult population that has ever existed. Welcome to the new era of older adulthood!

Indeed, we are in a season of vast changes, not only in America but throughout the world. In this chapter, we will look at this new reality from a variety of angles. This information is important for our ministries as we shall shortly see.

## LIFE EXPECTANCY

For one thing, life expectancy has grown dramatically. From the beginning to the end of the twentieth century, the life expectancy for white males grew from forty-seven years to seventy; for white females from forty-nine to eighty; for black males thirty-three to sixty-eight; and for black females thirty-five to seventy-five.[1] And, for the most part, life expectancy has increased by a few months each year of the twenty-first century.

There have been a number of factors contributing to these longer lives. Improvements in public health, including reduced pollution and sanitation have had their impact. Also, development in the infrastructure of societies has resulted in better distribution of fresh water. The discovery of antibiotics, development of vaccines, enhancement in education, and other advances in medical care contributed to this increased life expectancy. And then, good genes, a wise lifestyle, satisfying relationships, and a happy-positive outlook are among the contributing factors to increased years.

As to the future of life expectancy in the twenty-first century, there are two opposite views. On the one hand, there is excitement about where extension of life can lead. Sonya Collins asks, "Is 100 the New 80? What's It Take to Live Longer?" She notes that living into one's eighties and nineties is not that unusual and even the number of people who are 100 years of age or older has increased vastly—from 50,000 in 2,000 to 72,000 in 2015. That is still a minute minority among older adults, although it is "a whopping 43 percent" increase, she notes.[2]

On the other hand, the rate of life expectancy leveled in 2015 and declined in 2016, 2017, and 2018. Suicides and drug overdoses, connected to the opioid epidemic but not limited to it, are the main reasons for this decline. Why should people die seemingly needlessly with all the advances in medical sciences to sustain life? Close observers point to a loss of hope as a possible explanation among some people. This may come from loneliness, post-trauma distress among veterans and others, crises with relationships, substance use, jobs or unemployment frustration, or finances. Such may be seen as "deaths of despair."[3] In 2019, life expectancy again increased by a few months.

Older males are one of the populations where the suicide rate is growing the fastest. Again, this is a small minority, but still a concern for those who would know and care about older adults more effectively. Those of us in ministry need ask, what makes for hope and what makes for despair among those we serve? We also need to consider, who is at risk?

An equally important question is, how will our ministries respond to the much greater numbers of older adults among us?

## THE POPULATION DISTRIBUTION

This overall life expectancy increase leads to another unique aspect of aging today—the sheer volume of older adults. Two-thirds of all the people who have ever lived past 65 are alive today! In 1900, there were 3.1 million people in America over 65, in 2017 50.9 million! This growth is both in raw numbers and proportion of the American population—from 4.1 percent of the population in 1900 to 15.6 percent in 2017. Further, this is expected to grow to 21.7 percent of the population by 2040.[4]

When the growth of the numbers of elders is considered alongside the vastly decreased birthrate, another vast difference comes into view. That is the change of population distribution. As Paul Taylor of the Pew Research

Organization puts it, "Demographic transformations are dramas in slow motion." He notes two such dramas happening at the same time. One is that our population is "going gray." The other is that the American population which was 85 percent white in in 1960 will be only 43 percent white by 2060. While we were once a black and white country, "Now, we're a rainbow."[5] Both of these changes are important. However, in this book, we will concentrate on the changed aging phenomenon.

Population distribution used to be seen as a "pyramid." When putting the number of persons of each age—from birth to death—on a graph, it would resemble a pyramid, the largest numbers being the young, and the smallest, the old. Figure 1.1 shows the population distribution in 1960.

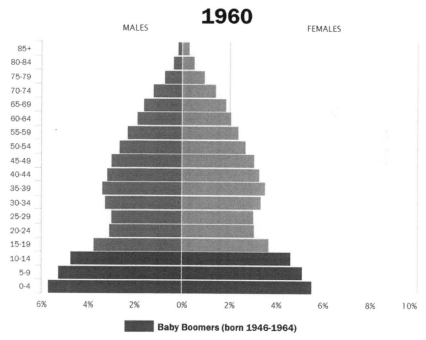

Figure 1.1  **Population Distribution 1960.** *Source: Pew Research 2014,* https://www.pewresearch.org/next-america/.

Now, when the numbers of each age are graphed, it comes out more nearly as a rectangle, with roughly the same numbers in each age range. There is even a term for this, the "rectangularization of population distribution." Simply put, today there are as many seventy-year-olds as seventeen-year-olds.

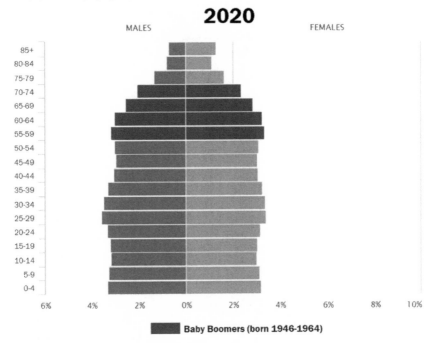

*U.S. Age Pyramid Becomes a Rectangle*
U.S. population by age group, 1950-2060

**Figure 1.2   Population Distribution 2020.** *Source: Pew Research 2014,* https://www. pewresearch.org/next-america/.

Figure 1.2 shows how population distribution looks in 2020.

This "rectangularization" will become even more pronounced over coming years. In 2060, there will be nearly as many eighty- to eighty-five-year-olds, as birth to five-year-olds. The present and future age distribution poses many public policy issues such as how to support and sustain a population so distributed. We will leave those for others to explore as we look at the ministry implications of these changes for us in the present.

## THE COHORTS AMONG OLDER ADULTS

However, of course not all older adults are alike. There are some broad distinctions among them that are a beginning to understanding the vast variety. One of these is the concept of "cohorts."

The word "cohort" basically describes a group of people with a common statistical characteristic. In life stage conversations, a cohort denotes a group of people who lived in the same period of time and experienced the historical events that occurred during that time.

In the present, there are some of three different cohorts among us elders:

- the "GI Generation" better known by Tom Brokaw's term "Greatest Generation" born 1905–1925 and quickly fading from us;
- the "Silent Generation" born 1925–1945; and
- the "Baby Boomer Generation," born 1946–1964.

We older adults have many differences among us, and some of them come from being a part of one of these cohorts. Two recent experiences made me aware of this. In the men's group at our retirement community, among the twenty or twenty-five of us, there are three "GI Generation" members, all veterans of World War II, particularly in the Pacific theatre.

On a recent Memorial Day, we were discussing the decision to drop the Atomic Bomb in 1945. I remember news of those bombs and the end of World War II from my childhood. I said to these three, "Perhaps it was necessary to drop one A bomb to show the threat if they did not surrender. But was it necessary to drop the second one?" My assumption would have been "no," but all three vigorously argued that it was necessary. They spoke of the great dread all felt about the then imminent invasion of Japan with every citizen armed and trained to resist and kill the invaders. In their view, the bombs prevented a prolonged bloody battle that would have taken tens of thousands of lives. However, to their surprise, when they speak to high school or college classes, they hardly ever find a person who thinks we should have dropped even one—different ages, different experiences, different conclusions. I should add that one of those veterans, a friendly and outgoing man proud of his naval service and in his mid-nineties, died in his sleep a few weeks after that conversation.

My other experience came when I attended a panel discussion of Wendy Holden's book *Born Survivors*.[6] This is a World War II Holocaust account of three imprisoned young mothers who, near the end of the war and in terrible circumstances, gave birth to their children. She relates how they courageously cared for those babies just before and at about the time of their camps being liberated. She also tells of the survival of those children. A panelist, Mark, was one of those three babies. Another panelist said to him, "You are the youngest Holocaust survivor." Mark is seventy-three years old, a retired emergency room physician. This hit me hard because my studies of the Holocaust have deeply impacted me and led to the conviction it was a horror that must not be forgotten. If the youngest survivor is seventy-three, most of the older Holocaust survivors have already died or will soon be leaving us just like their contemporaries in "the Greatest Generation." Those grim lessons of history will need a new generation of interpreters who were not eyewitnesses. These experiences point to the passing of a cohort, with many who had convictions based on their firsthand encounter of World War II and its many terrors and atrocities.

My cohort is next. As mentioned, we were born in 1925–1945. We are described as the "Silent Generation" although I prefer to think of us as the "Drought, Depression, and War Babies." We grew up in a time of scarcity, saving, and—during World War II—rationing. Because of the nature of those times, we were, therefore, a very small cohort, overshadowed by the generations before us and after us. Out of our early experiences, many of us are frugal and conservative financially.

With our small numbers, demographers do not often subdivide us. And yet those born in the first half of this period may have more vivid memories of the droughts and sandstorms of the 1930s and the rationing of the 1940s. Those born in the second half of this period may have been youths and young adults in the post-war boom that followed World War II.

The next generation/cohort of elders is the Baby Boomers, born 1946–1964. This population explosion following World War II has had overwhelming impact on each life stage through which it has passed. As Ken Dychtwald put it, "The Baby Boom was born to become an age wave." He visualizes the demands and changes it has made on the various agencies, institutions, and life stages it has passed through. He does so with an uncomplimentary but vivid metaphor—"like a pig moving through a python."[7]

Baby Boomers arrive in elder years probably in better health and vigor, and certainly appearing so. Dychtwald describes them as "a generation of Peter Pans." He notes that on the average, this generation went to school longer, married later, had children later, and so arrive at some generation "markers" of aging ten or more years later than previous generations. And so, continuing this pattern, when they reach the age in years usually thought of as "old" (say sixty-five), they do not look or self-identify as old.

> There are only three ages in Hollywood—Babe, District Attorney, and Driving Miss Daisy.
>
> —Goldie Hawn

He tells of speaking at a conference of recent retirees, that he describes as "energetic and attractive." He asked them what age people were before becoming "old" and their consensus was seventy-five. He asked them, "You believe that your generation is growing old more youthfully than older people at any previous time in history?" They responded with a huge round of applause. He continued "So you believe that because of things like medical science and better self-care, you are getting older later than you imagined you would?" Another round of applause. He then asked, "So then, I guess you wouldn't mind not getting your old age entitlements until you're seventy-five?" The response was stony silence.[8] He has repeated this exercise with other older Boomer audiences with exactly the same response.

And yet, there is much variety within the Boomers as well. Part of this may come from where they are within this huge cohort. Richard Gentzler notes that to understand boomers, it might be wise to divide them into two subgroups or cohorts: leading-edge boomers (born 1946–1954) and trailing-edge boomers (born 1955–1964).

Some characteristics often noted in leading-edge boomers include "individualism experimentation, anti-war activities, and civil rights movements." They may be more "left of center" as regards social, political, and religious issues. As I write in 2020, this sub-cohort is already past the age of sixty-five and into the retirement years as often conceived.

Trailing-edge boomers are often seen as having "general cynicism, less optimism, fewer opportunities." They became young adults in a time of economic decline, and a tighter labor market. They may have been drawn to the "Jesus movement," and may be more right of center as regards social, political, and religious topics than the earlier boomers. They will be the next sub-cohort to enter into the sixty-five and above period of life.[9]

Of course, all these statements about cohorts and sub-cohorts are generalizations, and as one of my professors used to say, "All generations are false, including this one." There are multiple variations as to how persons experience the life and times of their cohort.

In their book *Third Calling: What Are You Doing the Rest of Your Life?* Richard and Leona Bergstrom conclude with a challenge to their fellow boomers, "We're a rebellious bunch, and together we just might change what growing older means."[10] I'm sure they will, but at the same time will have many of the same experiences and issues of older people from time immemorial.

I recently heard a story that describes the differences among those in the aging spectrum. A retired early baby boomer moved into an established retirement community. After living there for a short time, she became aware that the forced air heating system was irritatingly loud, both in one's apartment and in the dining area. She spoke to the administrators and was told nothing could be done about that. She did not accept that and kept on protesting. Her career had been related to engineering firms, and so she contacted her engineering friends for guidance. Eventually, she persisted until the problem was solved. Older residents were delighted. They had complained about the sound for years but accepted it when the administration said nothing could be done. A boomer refused to accept that answer.

The present and future populations of older adults will have great variety and differences among them, some of it arising out of the fact that as many as three different cohorts will be in that life stage at the same time.

It is important to understand how significant cohort sensitivity is in ministering with older adults. I recall a conversation from years ago. A year or two after I had left my first full-time pastorate (a church in a county seat town in rural South Dakota) that I served in the early 1960s, the church invited all former pastors back to celebrate an anniversary. Only two of us former pastors came, a man in his sixties, and I in my early thirties. One time during that weekend, the two of us and the present pastor—in his twenties—were visiting. The older pastor commented, "When I was here, we lived through the drought and the depression." The younger pastor snapped back, "And we've been living through it ever since!" He was probably thinking of the financial conservatism, "stinginess," and caution of his older members. I now see this as an example of failed communication across cohorts, something that may happen in various ways in churches and other ministries.

## LIFE STAGES WITHIN THE OLDER ADULT YEARS

Another way to view older adults is considering the life-stage variations among them. Rather than historical context, this is to explore the experience of aging itself, its impact on physical health, relationships, and life management. Though many may think of "old age" as only one such period, there are at least two, perhaps more life stages among older adults.

Bernice Neugarten, a pioneer in the field of gerontology was one of the first to advocate sensitivity to the nuances and changes within the older adult years. In the 1970s, she started addressing the difference between being "young-old" and "old-old." Originally, she designated ages fifty-five to seventy-four as "young-old" but later changed that to sixty-five to seventy-four. She placed age seventy-five and beyond as "old-old." Further, she noted that economic status, health status, and more impacted the life of each older adult along this spectrum.[11]

Neugarten was born in 1936 and died in 2001. When she wrote of the older years in the 1970s, she was in the midst of the century that saw life expectancy and the numbers of older adults grow exponentially. As aging extends in time and expands in numbers, others have revised the way they see the life-stage experience of older adults.

In the early 1990s, Peter Laslett wrote *A Fresh Map of Life: The Emergence of the Third Age.* In that book, he noted that an individual may be seen as having several different ages, not entirely distinct from each other, and "related in slightly confusing ways." He spoke of the following: a calendar or chronological age; a biological age; a personal age; a social age (or even ages); and a subjective age.[12]

He pointed out that we largely think of life in three huge chapters: childhood-youth, the chapter of education and preparation; young and middle adulthood, the chapter of work and achievement; and older adulthood, the chapter of retirement, decline, and death.

Instead, Laslett advocated "a fresh map of life" that he conceived in this way:

- First, an era of dependence, socialization, immaturity, and education.
- Second an era of independence, maturity, responsibility, earning, and saving.
- Third an era of personal fulfillment (early elder years)
- Then, finally, a fourth era of dependence, decrepitude, and death.[13]

As with Neugarten he divided older adulthood into two ages: an age of fulfillment, growth, and community enrichment; and an age of decline and death. He, therefore, suggested that the task of persons in this third age of fulfillment is do everything they can to extend this period and make the fourth period as brief as possible. This, he said, includes continued activity of the body and mind, and dealing with health issues, which include in his words avoiding "the appalling dangers of smoking."

And, far from withdrawing into their own world, Laslett advocated that adults in this age of fulfillment have a civic function and responsibility "founding, shaping, sustaining, and extending their own institutions" for the benefit of society. With the huge numbers in this life stage, it is important not to be a liability, but rather a resource of the renewal of our communities and world.

One of the elders Roland Martinson interviewed, playfully described the stages of older adult life "go-go, go-slow, no-go." The boundary between vigorous old age and declining old age is not always clear. However, as another elder told Roland Martinsen "health is the 'trump card' in old age, and it's always in play."[14]

In my early retirement employment as a seminary professor, I discovered how true this is when a minor surgical procedure became complicated. My urologist recommended a procedure to reduce the size of my prostate with the least invasive laser method. He said I would go home five to six hours after the surgery. I would wear a catheter for a week, but then could return to my regular activities. I agreed and scheduled it for a week when there were no classes for me to teach.

The reality was different from what the doctor described. I kept bleeding inside and outside the catheter. There were two return trips to the hospital emergency room, three trips in all to the operating room, oxygen, transfusions, and days in the hospital.

Procedures and convalescence stretched into weeks. For a time, I could not leave the bed nor walk without assistance. For even longer I could not be left alone, drive, or do so many basic things for myself. Friends or family were needed to "Dick sit."

My world shrank from planning next year's classes, conferences, and writing projects to this week's doctor appointments, medications, and naps. I experienced old-old for a month or so. Gradually, some of the symptoms receded. Bit by bit, I regained a little more stamina, limited driving privileges, a visit to my classes, and then full time but reduced responsibilities.

Eventually, I was back to "normal," but that experience did not leave me unchanged. I had a preview of "old-old" and did not like it! I experienced what I should have known, that "young-old" will not last forever, and that it can change at any time. I also re-resolved to tend to my own health practices to prolong young and middle old times as long as possible. Even so, the health resilience that helped me recover in my sixties slowly declines as I age.

## ECONOMIC VARIATIONS AMONG THE ELDERS

There is another variation that cuts across the cohorts and life stages—that is the wide variety of economic situations. We all age and will, in time, need more resources for medical care and other caregiving provisions. Some of elders will be able to afford this with no dent on our standard of living; others of us will not.

The National Council on Aging noted that almost 75 percent of Social Security recipients aged sixty-five or older depend on Social Security for all or most of their income, approximately $15,000 a year. These persons will be hard pressed or unable to afford doctors, medicines, hospitals, or therapies.

The Council also notes that over 23 million Americans aged 60+ are economically insecure, which they define at having income at or below 250 percent of the federal poverty level. This would translate to $28, 725 for a single person.

In a survey of a representative group of persons in this income range, they learned that nearly half (46 percent) of low- and moderate-income seniors are not confident that their income will be enough to meet their monthly expenses over the next five to ten years. Nor are they confident they will be able to meet medical expense or pay for any other unexpected emergencies.[15]

Sensitive ministries with elders need to be cognizant not only of cohorts and life stages but also of the wide variety of economic situations and possible dilemmas some older adults are facing.

## GENDER DIFFERENCES

Further, as Louise Aronson notes, "Old age is profoundly gendered."[16] While women are 51 percent of the overall population, they are 57 percent of people over sixty-five, 68 percent of those over eighty-five, and 83 percent of centenarians. Thus, advanced older age issues are often more women's health issues than for men who may have died earlier.

For now, we simply note this discrepancy. We will explore what it means to our ministries in the next chapter.

## MINISTRY IMPLICATIONS

What clues or insights for ministry might we take from this first look? If we take to heart the population explosion of older adults, their cohorts, and the life stages within the older years, where does it lead? It might lead away from disappointment of serving a shrinking community of mostly old people to awareness of exciting possibilities.

It opens new opportunities for ministry and service. Among these older adults, there are many talents and much energy to be enlisted. Other agencies see this and are responding. For example, the retirement residential communities are urgently building to accommodate the coming increase. I hear financial staff where I live fervently working on building 100 or more apartments for independent senior living. They expect to have them sold before they are finished because—"ten thousand people turn sixty-five every day."

For another example, educational institutions are changing to respond to the shrinkage of available young adults and the expansion of older adults. For example, the University of Wisconsin's Institute on Aging's site notes, "Over the past 100 years, we have witnessed enormous change in the size of the aging population in the U.S.—from around 1 out of every 25 persons in the early 1900s to around 1 out of every 4 or 5 persons in the 21st century. Because adults represent the fastest growing segment of society our universities must provide leadership, training, and scientific advances to meet their diverse needs."[17]

Still another entity that is aware of and responsive to the growing population of older adults is the arts community. For example, consider the New

Horizons band and orchestra movement. In the early 1990s, founder Roy Ernst, Ph.D., had an idea at the Eastman School of Music in Rochester, New York. As he anticipated the Baby Boomer age wave, he founded a band for retired people, or those about to be. Persons with no previous training would be welcome. He believed that anyone would be able to learn to play music at a level that will bring a sense of accomplishment along with the ability to play in a group. His original little band with thirty players has now grown into a movement with at least 10,000 musicians and 215 bands in the United States and several other countries.[18]

I joined a New Horizons band in Roeland Park, Kansas and enjoyed it tremendously for several years. When I told my director I was moving, he asked me to promise to find a New Horizons band in my new location, and I did so. It has been the door to creativity, friendship, growth, and feeling at home in a new community. I gladly pay the fees to belong, because it offers something very precious to me, an older adult.

Retirement communities, universities, and music organizations view the present and future older adult population as challenge and opportunity. So can the church and related agencies. A possibility of new and different ministries may come into view. There is a brighter and more enduring future for effective ministry with elders than previously thought. In other chapters, I will describe what some of these possible ministries are and tell the stories of churches that have discovered ways to do this very thing.

Further, this information may also be of help in establishing rapport, visiting, and learning about the older adults you know now. There might be topics of experience and history where you might learn something new. One of my failures—there was a quiet, somewhat taciturn older man in one of my congregations. Only when he died, did I learn from his family that not only was he a World War II veteran, he had been part of Patton's army that battled, liberated, and marched across Europe. Would he have opened up and talked about his experiences if asked? Sadly, I will never know.

Will the ministries and programs you plan serve all older adults or a more limited life stage or cohort? Only those in your setting can answer that. Possibly some ministries are age specific and others are intergenerational— even beyond the life stages of the old.

I do remember a church older adult group that was struggling. For a long time, they had met for a potluck meal, conversation, and a program several times a year. For each program, three or four members would set up the tables, make coffee, clean up, and put things away afterward. But this was getting harder and harder as members grew older and frailer.

Each meeting they would lament, this was probably the last time they would be able to meet. They brushed off my suggestions that the church custodian could help with set up and putting things away. But they hoped that some church members on the verge of retiring would join and help out.

However, when the newly retired persons met to plan, they were not at all interested in the older group. They wanted outings, retreats, mission trips—active and energetic experiences. Each group and each cohort will have to find their way for themselves. And, if we are wise, we will be sensitive and resourceful to aid that search.

Some observing and listening are in order. But again, doing that is not as simple as might appear. In the next chapter, we will explore some of those barriers.

## FOR REFLECTING AND CONVERSING

1. How do the national statistics on aging as reported in this chapter relate to your community? Do you have a smaller proportion or greater proportion of adults in those years? What, if any, are your hunches about older adults where you live and what care or ministries might be welcome?
2. Where do you feel your ministry with older adults is strongest? Where are you puzzled or discouraged? What do older adults in your community wish their religious leaders knew about them?
3. I told my story of slipping into an older life stage with an unexpected surgery complication. Have you had similar experiences? Have persons with whom you minister? What might be the most helpful care in such times?
4. Where are the resources and who are the persons that can give you a clearer comprehension of the size, makeup, and interests of older adults in your community?
5. Did you hear any invitations for new ministries in this overview? If so, what are they?

## NOTES

1. "1900–2000: Changes in Life Expectancy in the United States," accessed January 4, 2020, https://www.seniorliving.org/history/1900-2000-changes-life-expectancy-united-states/.

2. Sonya Collins, "Is 100 the New 80? What's It Take to Live Longer?" *WebMD News*, accessed January 7, 2019, https://www.webmd.com/healthy-aging/news/2018 0920/is-100-the-new-80-whats-it-take-to-live-longer.

3. Mike Stobbe, "US Life Expectancy Dips," AP accessed at *Wisconsin State Journal* November 23, 2018, A8.

4. "A Profile of Older Americans, 2018," accessed March 23, 2020, https://ac l.gov/sites/default/files/Aging%20and%20Disability%20in%20America/2018Older AmericansProfile.pdf.

5. Paul Taylor, "The Next America," April 10, 2014, accessed February 28, 2020, https://www.pewresearch.org/next-america/#Two-Dramas-in-Slow-Motion.

6. Wendy Holden, *Born Survivors: Three Young Mothers and Their Extraordinary Story of Courage, Defiance, and Hope* (New York: Harper Perennial, 2015).

7. Ken Dychtwald, *Age Power: How the 21st Century Will Be Ruled by the New Old* (New York: Jeremy P. Tarcher/Putnam, 1999), 77, 58.

8. Dychtwald, *Age Power*, 86, 92–93.

9. Richard H. Gentzler, Jr., *An Age of Opportunity: Intentional Ministry By, With, and For Older Adults* (Nashville: Discipleship Resources, 2018), 79.

10. Richard Bergstrom and Leona Bergstrom, *Third Calling: What Are You Doing the Rest of Our Life?* (Edmonds, WA: Re-Ignite, A Division of ChurchHealth, 2016), 159.

11. Robert Binstock, "In Memoriam: Bernice L. Neugarten," *The Gerontologist* 42, no. 2 (2002): 149–51.

12. Peter Laslett, *A Fresh Map of Life: The Emergence of the Third Age* (Cambridge: Harvard University Press, 1991), 24.

13. Laslett, *A Fresh Map of Life*, 4.

14. Roland B. Martenson, *Elders Rising: The Promise and Peril of Aging* (Minneapolis: Fortress Press, 2018), 76, 206.

15. Information came from the National Council on Aging, https://www.ncoa.org /economic-security/money-management/, accessed November 17, 2019.

16. Louise Aronson, *Elderhood: Redefining Aging, Transforming Medicine, Reimagining Life* (New York: Bloomsbury Publishing, 2019), 335.

17. "The Challenges of our Aging Society," accessed November 15, 2009, http:// www.aging.wisc.edu.

18. "Music for Life: The Story of New Horizons," accessed March 23, 2020, https://www.wxxi.org/musicforlife.

## Chapter 2

# Sooner or Later, Have an "Attitude Adjustment" Time

Do not speak harshly to an older man but speak to him as a father, to younger men as brothers, to older women as mothers, to younger women as sisters – with absolute purity.

—I Timothy 5:1-2

If you are eager to read about ministry needs and opportunities with older adults, you may want to skip over this chapter until later. However, it will be wise to read it some time. I am going to discuss some of the barriers that get into the way of elders' full acceptance in society. These are also matters that may diminish effective ministry with older adults as well.

### FIRST IMPRESSIONS

When starting to visit with older adults hoping to know their world and experiences better, it may be more difficult than expected. You may call on a frail older adult with the best of intention but find it hard going.

A number of things may get in the way. We olders may have trouble hearing or understanding you. We may not be able to keep up with the speed at which you talk. Or your accent which may not be noticeable to most people may affect our comprehension. A fairly common ailment among the aging is not only hearing loss but decreased aural word comprehension.

Or, you may have trouble understanding us. We may converse at a much slower pace. There may be moments, perhaps several moments before we speak, and we may speak slowly, hesitantly. We may have a hard time finding a word we want to use. You may want to fill in words or finish our sentences for us, but that is the last thing we want. Our voice may be weak, even hard for you, a younger visitor to hear. It may be somewhat monotone so that any moods or mood change are hard to discern. Some of us older persons have less affect in our speaking, and so it may be hard to know if you are making contact.

We may have constant pain and appear crabby or morose. You might be unsure whether to stay or leave. It may be helpful to ask if now or some other time is a good time for a visit. You see, one of the greatest pains of old age is loneliness. However, our appearance and difficulty communicating may drive away persons like you whom we would like to be our friends.

You may find it extremely hard to find common ground. It may be difficult to intuit the limitations of our world if we are in a senior center or confined to an assisted living facility. You may not be able to imagine what you can tell us about your life and activities that would interest us. Further, you may be at a loss as to what to ask us about our life experiences in a rather confined environment.

Some of us may have conditions of health that a new visitor may find it hard to overcome—shaking, affected speech, respiration assistance (oxygen), hearing aids that might not work or might squeal, wheelchair, or walker. In some of the care areas for the frailest of older adults, there may be scents that can be distracting—disinfectant, or urine, or something else.

If you ask us how we are feeling, we might tell you—perhaps in much more detail than you care to hear. Health is a constant concern for us. It is one of our adventures/battles in our time of life. And so, we elders frequently compare experiences with each other when we have a common health problem. We might support each other through cataract surgery, for example, talking through each step.

Recently I saw a young pastor on a late afternoon. He looked exhausted and somewhat depressed. I asked him what was up. He said he had just been to the hospital to call on an older man in his church. "When I asked him how he was feeling, he responded, 'To answer that, I'll have to take you back to 91,'—and he did, describing everything that happened to his health since then in great detail!" Yes, at times ministry with us older adults is time and energy demanding.

## THE CULTURAL CONTEXT OF AGING

In addition to those difficulties of making contact with persons, there are forces at work within our culture that challenge and hamper the place of older adults in our society and culture. Years ago, May Sarton noted, "The trouble is, old age is not interesting until one gets there. It's a foreign country with an unknown language to the young and even to the middle aged."[1]

We may nod our heads in agreement with Sarton, but then another question occurs to us. Why? Why are older adults not seen as interesting? That is not true in many other cultures where older adults are respected and revered.

Fifty years ago, the pioneering gerontologist Robert N. Butler observed that aging is the neglected stepchild of the human life cycle. In 1968, he coined the word "ageism" and described it with these words:

> Ageism can be seen as a process of systematic stereotyping of and discrimination against people because they are old, just as racism and sexism accomplish this with skin color and gender. Old people are categorized as senile, rigid in thought and manner, old-fashioned in morality and skills. . . . Ageism allows the younger generations to see older people as different from themselves; thus, they subtly cease to identify with their elders as human beings.[2]

He further observed, "Negative attitudes toward the old range from pity and infantilization to avoidance or direct hostility."[3]

More than fifty years later, the World Health Organization is addressing this still urgent issue. Their web page provides this overview:

> Ageism is the stereotyping, prejudice, and discrimination against people on the basis of their age. Ageism is widespread and an insidious practice which has harmful effects on the health of older adults. For older people, ageism is an everyday challenge. Overlooked for employment, restricted from social services and stereotyped in the media, ageism marginalises and excludes older people in their communities.
>
> Ageism is everywhere, yet it is the most socially "normalized" of any prejudice and is not widely countered—like racism or sexism. These attitudes lead to the marginalisation of older people within our communities and have negative impacts on their health and well-being.[4]

Other concerned scholars have noted the truth of Butler's (and the World Health Organization's) insight and have given it newer names and descriptions. In her earlier work *Another Country*, Mary Pipher described this cultural attitude as "xenophobia"—fear and suspicion of those who live in the country of the old.[5] In her later work *Women Rowing North* that she wrote particularly for and on behalf of her fellow aging women, she calls it "gerontophobia." She notes that a Yale School of Public Health study investigated attitudes of twenty- to twenty-nine-year-olds toward the aging. They discovered that 75 percent on those surveyed denigrated older people. Pipher goes on to note that "ultimately ageism is a prejudice against one's own future self."[6] However, we older adults continue to contribute to our society, strengthen the economy with our buying power, and we vote. We deserve to be treated better.

Tom Koch, eldercare advocate and researcher elaborates:

> We do not like our seniors, nor do we understand them. They are wrinkled, shrunken in stature, and too often they speak in dry and querulous voices.

Our assumptions of physical beauty and social responsibility are violated by the elderly, who rarely work and are free of the obligations that plague us younger adults.[7]

And so, rather than older adults being the wise guides for preserving a culture's values and guiding the young in difficult decisions, something has changed. Now we have become marginal citizens of a new and continually changing world that we navigate only with some confusion and with great difficulty. Pipher observes, "While adolescence is about the loss of childhood, old age is about the loss of adult status and power."[8]

Our families in the generations after us may be kind and caring and have fond memories of us from their childhoods. However, rarely are we seen as the ones who have the gifts of tradition, wisdom, faith, ethics, and values to guide them in their course.

If we forget this, media and other popular culture will remind us! Seldom are older adults portrayed as wise and compassionate. Too often we are seen as silly, petty, childish, toothless, and sexless.

It is worth asking why, in a culture with so many more older people than previously, do we have so few elders?—elders, that is, who are seen as wise leaders, educators, and counselors of the young and of society as a whole.

By contrast, Joe Starita describes the place of old people among the Lakota tribe, "The Lakota believe that if the old do not stay connected to the young, the culture will disintegrate. Older people tell stories that teach lessons and keep the culture alive. Because wisdom is highly valued among the Lakota, the older people are, the more they are loved. Older equals wiser equals more respected."[9]

I experienced similar respect and love for old people during my sabbatical stay in various countries of Southeast Asia.

## COMPLICATIONS

But it is even more complicated than we have observed so far. When Butler listed ageism as similar to sexism and racism, there is another sad truth implied: people may be victims of more "isms" than one!

We need to unpack these words—ageism, sexism, racism. It is important to acknowledge that while engaging in any of these "isms," one does not have to have hard feelings, conscious disdain, or recognized prejudice toward the other.

One or more of these "isms" can exist inside of you or me who see ourselves as kind and well intentioned. Without much thought, we have simply accepted the privileges and powers that go with being on the favored side of any one of these. And so, without thinking, we unconsciously buy into cultural assumptions and myths.

Let's take a brief look at where at least two "isms" come together.

## Ageism and Sexism

Ann, a seventy-year-old retired social worker told Karen Scheib, "Old women are invisible. Don't you know that? . . . Really, I mean, if I walk down the street in any town, most people—men and women up to I'd say the age of fifty-five to sixty—don't notice me. I am invisible."[10] In her research, Scheib found this experience often among older women. She discerned it in church as well as elsewhere. It leads her to believe that age is largely a negative term in American culture.

Another of her elderly interviewees told her, "As you get older you cease to exist in the eyes of some younger people; you become invisible. No one seems interested in who you are or what you do. It is disconcerting."[11]

Scheib speaks of aging, particularly of women aging as a "social construction." That is, "old age" is not a neutral term, but reflects cultural assumptions and values, that in turn have been influenced by other social structures such as market economy, public policy, academic disciplines, and popular culture.[12]

As Mary Pipher puts it,

> "Old women in America suffer a social disease. For us ageism may be an even more serious challenge than aging. Our sexuality is mocked, our bodies are derided, and our voices are silenced."[13]

She points to birthday cards for older women as one example of how popular culture demeans older women. For they portray these women as "being senile, drinking too much, or being sexually over-the-hill or sexually insatiable."[14]

This is happening while, as we noted in the first chapter, older women are the true survivors among us. The ratio of women to men at the age of sixty-five is 118 to 100. At the age of eighty-five and above, the ratio is 237 to 100. Many of these women are not only survivors in age; they hold wisdom and prophetic fervor for the times in which they live.

---

There are six myths about old age:

1. That it is a disease, a disaster.
2. That we are mindless.
3. That we are sexless.
4. That we are useless.
5. That we are powerless.
6. That we are all alike.

—Maggie Kuhn, founder
of Gray Panthers

---

Maggie Kuhn, founder of the "Gray Panthers" observed "We who are old have nothing to lose! We have everything to gain by living dangerously! We can initiate change without jeopardizing jobs or family. We can be the risk-takers."[15]

If the present status of older women is a social construction, there can also be a social deconstruction and social reconstruction of this view. While it will not happen quickly or easily, a first step may be an attitude adjustment of church leaders who could claim the gifts of a growing population of elders, including the most enduring of all, the women.

## Ageism and Racism

Theologian Leah Schade has written of her discovery that she is a "recovering racist." She notes she grew up in a family and culture that assumed she was superior to people whose skin color was darker. She unwittingly and unconsciously developed a set of discriminatory attitudes based on these assumptions and perceptions. She notes "It was the water I swam in but was not conscious of."

Now with greater awareness, she notes,

Racism has to do with the *power* that is ascribed to me based on my white skin. I didn't ask for this power, and I may not always be conscious of it, but I have it nonetheless. It's granted to me through social structures and conventions as well as my having access to resources that are closed to others based on their skin color. This means that my personal racism is a manifestation of a systemic problem. Our entire culture and society are in need of recovery from racism.[16]

In chapter 1, we noted the rise in life expectancy in the twentieth century. There was discrepancy between Euro-Americans and Afro-Americans, larger at the beginning of the century than at the end, but still a discrepancy of several years. Indeed, all the variations in access to education, finance, power that are part of the racism, of which Schade writes, contribute to the difficulties of persons who are victims of ageism and racism at the same time. For example, a late twentieth-century study by the American Association of Retired Persons reported that one-third of elderly African Americans lived in poverty as compared to 11 percent of elderly whites. The same study pointed that the vast majority of African American Women (62 percent) live in poverty.[17]

African American churches are one place where the corrosive combination of ageism and racism is countered. Ann Streaty Wimberly points to two interrelated values that guide African American congregations as regards their elders. One is the *soul community* "To speak of the soul community is to speak of an African American community that operates from a sense of 'peoplehood' and an appreciation of shared history, shared culture and shared challenges." Hospitality, closeness, and bonds across generations come from this value.

The other value is *honor*. "To honor African American elders means to acknowledge the significance of their years and to treat them as persons of worth."[18] She notes that this honor takes the form of "three R's." The community honors elders "as *recipients* of care, as *repositories* of wisdom, and as *resourceful participants* in community life."[19] In this rich sense of community and honor, some of the blows of living in an ageist, racist culture, are lessened and managed.

In the edited volume I have been citing, *Honoring African American Elders: A Ministry in the Soul Community* there is perspective and guidance that proceeds from the heritage described above and moves into a new paradigm for ministry with older adults.

## AND SO

We have been exploring the distances between the generations, the difficulty in relating across these generations, and the varied barriers that make this problem even more difficult. The barriers ageism, sexism, and racism are real. It is difficult, yes, but not impossible to build bridges across these barriers. In our day, the effort to reach across these barriers can be richly rewarding for the persons on both sides. In the chapters that follow, we will spell out this possibility. For now, some self-reflection and analysis of the place of elders in the current culture and churches as well as first steps at learning and communicating will open the door.

## FOR REFLECTING AND CONVERSING

1. Where do you find yourself in this discussion of ageism? Did you recognize yourself at times? If so, where? Did you find yourself resisting? At what points?

2. Who, among the elders you know, is the easiest to know, to relate to? What makes that person that way? What can that person possibly help you with in relating to other older adults?

3. What breakthroughs have you experienced in relationships with older adults? What brought about the breakthrough? What were the gains for each of you? What insights do you gain from this experience?

4. What steps can you take to discover whether none, some, or much of this chapter is true about your community and your place of ministry?

5. Access this World Health Organization resource on "The Global Network for Age-friendly Cities and Communities: Looking back over the last decade, looking forward to the next"[20] What ideas or possibilities does it stir for you?

## NOTES

1. As quoted in Mary Pipher, *Another Country: Negotiating the Emotional Terrain of Our Elders* (New York: Riverhead Books, 1999), 15.

2. Robert N. Butler, *Why Survive? Being Old in America* (Baltimore: The Johns Hopkins University Press, 1975), 11–12.

3. Butler, *Why Survive?* 402.

4. "Aging and Life Course," accessed March 23, 2020, https://www.who.int/ageing/ageism/en/.

5. Pipher, *Another Country*, 39.

6. Mary Pipher, *Women Rowing North: Navigating Life's Currents and Flourishing as We Age* (New York: Bloomsbury Publishing, 2018), 30.

7. Tom Koch, *Age Speaks*, 1 as quoted in Karen Scheib, *Challenging Invisibility: Practices of Care with Older Women* (St. Louis: Chalice, 2004), 30.

8. Pipher, *Another Country*, 131.

9. As summarized by Pipher, *Another Country*, 42–43 from Joe Starita, *The Dull Knifes of Pine Ridge* (Lincoln, NE: Bison Books, 2002).

10. Scheib, *Challenging Invisibility*, 1.

11. Scheib, *Challenging Invisibility*, 1.

12. Scheib, *Challenging Invisibility*, 19.

13. Pipher, *Women Rowing North*, 27.

14. Pipher, *Women Rowing North*, 27.

15. "Maggie Kuhn Quotes," accessed August 24, 2019, https://www.thoughtco.com/maggie-kuhn-quotes-3525374.

16. "Hi, I'm Leah. I'm a Recovering Racist," accessed August 24, 2019, https://www.patheos.com/blogs/ecopreacher/2019/01/recovering-racist/?utm_source=Newsletter&utm_medium=email&utm_campaign=Progressive+Christian&utm_content=43.

17. Anne Streaty Wimberly (ed.), *Honoring African American Elders: A Ministry in the Soul Community* (San Francisco: Jossey and Bass, 1997), 17.

18. Wimberly, *Honoring African American Elders*, xii.

19. Wimberly, *Honoring African American Elders*, 6, italics hers.

20. "The Global Network for Age-friendly Cities and Communities: Looking Back Over the Last Decade, Looking Forward to the Next," accessed March 23, 2020, https://extranet.who.int/agefriendlyworld/.

# Chapter 3

# Discern

## Profiles in Courage, Caring, Coping, and Creativity

The righteous flourish like the palm tree, and grow like a cedar in Lebanon.

In old age they still produce fruit; they are always green and full of sap.

—Psalm 92:12, 14

Why did Grandma Moses start painting at the age of seventy-six? (Because her hands were too arthritic to embroider anymore.)

Where did Colonel Sanders get the money to start his chicken business? (His first social security check.)

There are lists aplenty of what extraordinary older adults accomplished in their advanced years, for example:

Gladys Burrill ran and completed a marathon at the age of ninety-two.

Teiichi Igarashi climbed Mt. Fuji at hundred.

William Ivy Baldwin tightrope walked across a canyon at eighty-two.

Diana Nyad swam from Cuba to Florida at sixty-four.

Peter Roget invented the thesaurus at seventy-three.[1]

Such lists are fun and may challenge some of the stereotypes of aging. However, as an elder among elders, I am not so interested in those distant and huge achievements. Rather, I am moved when I see the courage of persons who cope with their physical frailties creatively and with a minimum of complaint. I am touched by those who offer love and support to neighbors as they walk through pain and loss. I am inspired by those who find some way to keep serving a person or a cause they value. To me they are, to borrow John Kennedy's title, "Profiles in Courage" through their coping, their creativity, their caring. In this chapter, I will tell you about some of these people I have met and others I read about. As you read these stories, look around you and take note of the profiles in courage you see in your life and work.

## PROFILES IN COPING

When I came to live in a retirement community with several levels of care, I came to experience many people on walkers or in wheelchairs (mostly motorized, a few propelled by a helper). This has been a learning experience for me. It used to be when I saw a person with a walking aid, I wondered if I should do something to help. Here, I sense, people will care for these matters themselves unless they ask for help. Only once did I give some help without being asked. A small group of us had been taken by the bus to an outdoor band concert. When it was time to leave, the bus was in a different place to leave—up a fairly steep grassy slope. I sensed a woman straining to make it up, and so, fearful she might fall backward, I put my hands on her back and lent some support and strength. She thanked me.

I see much courage and coping here, and some of it is people on walkers. (The most common walkers here have either two or four wheels.) There are people who walk very slowly, perhaps painfully, but walk and walk and keep walking because they know if they quit walking, they will not be able to any-more. Often, on the way to the dining hall, we pass a woman, moving ever so slowly with small careful steps. We may already be seated and have ordered our food by the time she arrives to do the same.

People are creative with the decorations on their walkers and the way they use them. They pick up takeout food and put it on their device to carry it back to their rooms. One person takes both her meal and her neighbor's back to their apartments. Others pick up mail including packages at the post office in our building. If they see that a neighbor has a package, they may pick that up also and deliver it to their door. Our ninety-year-old baritone horn playing partner, Jean, loads her baritone in its case on her walker to come to practice or performance. These walkers can also provide room for all the things a woman once carried in her purse and more. One woman calls her walking aid her "wheelbarrow." Indeed, people use their walkers to take their gardening tools out to their gardening plot and their harvest back. Persons also usher at chapel using their walkers as they pass out bulletins, seat late worshippers, and take up the morning offering.

There are also wheelchairs mostly the electric motorized type. One such driver has a creative touch with his. He comes down to the dining hall for takeout food to his room. But since it would not be convenient to hold it on his lap, he has re-bent a clothes hanger and devised a wire hook on the back of his wheelchair. The dining room people put his food in a plastic bag with a loop on the top, and they hang it on the hook so he can take the meal up the elevator and back to his room.

## CONTENDING WITH ILLNESS-DISABILITY

I see courage and creativity as people contend with emerging health problems. Perhaps this issue can be dealt with through physical therapy or other treatment. Or it may require a more permanent adjustment to a new and changed reality.

From time to time, I see a woman who is losing her sight. She still gamely works at finding her way around with the support of her friends. The other day, she came down to the mail boxes the same time I did. I stood aside so she could—by touch—determine which was her mailbox. She took out her key, used her fingers to find the keyhole on her mailbox, after a couple tries put the key in the slot, turned the key, and opened the door—to find no mail at all that day! With a smile and a little huff, she turned around to go her way.

### Clifton

Louise Aronson tells of Clifton Fadiman, another person who lost his sight. He was a voracious reader and literary critic. He did not think life was worth living without his sight. A short time later, he attended a program that showed visually impaired persons strategies for independence. That was probably one of the most interesting days of his life. He was guided into ways to do much of what he enjoyed most.

He lived many more years. After he died, his daughter reflected that the period between his first low vision class and his final illness was one of the happiest of his life. Following the creative lead of those classes, he kept his mind agile by learning how to be blind. His daughter reflected, "He had considered himself a coward. Now he knew he wasn't."[2]

### Jean

Another person who inspires me is Jean, as I mentioned, one of our baritone horn trio. Jean had a ninetieth birthday last year. As part of the family's celebration of that, our trio played for a morning worship at her daughter's Methodist Church. Sometime after that she had what was described as a TIA, a ministroke. She felt she could no longer be an organist for one of the Sunday chapel services each month as she had done for nineteen years. She also told us, her trio mates, that she was through with baritone and could play it no more.

In the meantime, our chaplain had invited us to play for the Easter service. The other trio member, Russ invited Jean to come and listen to our practices and offer suggestions. He also kept Jean informed of our rehearsal times. Eventually she came to a practice session and sat there, listening without speaking. After a couple weeks of that, she showed up with her baritone and played along. She played with us on Easter Sunday, played her parts loud and clear—again with some her proud family there to support her. It was an Easter experience to have her back from that dark valley, joyously playing the magnificent music of the season.

## Agnes

Elizabeth MacKinlay, nurse and Anglican priest saw this courage in Agnes, who has diabetes and had a stroke about ten years earlier. At the time of the stroke, she was unconscious for three weeks and emerged with a right sided paralysis. Nevertheless, she went through a long rehabilitation, which she admits "was a bit hard" and eventually did learn to walk again. While recovering, she was helped by the support of a daughter who came and helped her with showers and feeding. Despite the long rehabilitation, she still was not well enough to be able to go home.

Agnes described her struggle to get well again, "Oh yes, I don't believe in sitting down and doing nothing [laughs] mainly because out at [the aged care facility] there was a man living here." She tells of the courage of this man who lost a leg but struggled back so that "he could walk around and dance and do everything."

Agnes has made her peace with not being able to live independently. Even with her diabetes and disabilities from her stroke, she is a person who finds meaning in life, laughs a lot, and showed great resilience. She has found many things she enjoys in the nursing home, most notably the crafts activities and visits from her daughter. MacKinlay reflects "This sense of resilience is a vital and perhaps elusive component in the mix that makes for well-being of any individual." Agnes has suffered much and still laughs and brings friendship to others—a person to be respected and admired.[3]

## David S.

David S. had been a Lutheran missionary, teaching Bible and Hebrew in many countries of the world. In his retirement years, he experienced ALS, "Lou Gehrig's disease," and initially, it took his speech away from him. For a time after that, he remained mobile and able to attend groups and activities. He bravely came to our men's group and participated in our conversations, carrying a small white board, marking pen, and eraser cloth to make his distinctive contributions. A disability that would cause many people to withdraw did not hold him back from full participation in a variety of activities, always entering in and contributing in his own way.

David died, recently. At his funeral, his pastor told us that David had designed the entire service. The sermon included several of the devotions from a book he had written. At the end of the service everyone was given a copy of that book, *Arrows of Light.*[4] We left the service remembering a person who was faithful to his calling and lived it to the very end.

## CARING FOR A PARTNER

### Lorraine

I see costly caring in many couples. It takes many forms. Our neighbor Lorraine's husband has been in the assisted living facility for at least two years. Occasionally she brought him in a wheelchair to some social events, but he was almost totally deaf and found it hard to relate. She spent her entire days with him in his care unit, and then would return to her apartment in the evening to wash his clothes. Recently her husband died, after a few weeks on hospice. He was loved and faithfully cared for to the end of his days. Now, in addition to grieving, she has another adjustment to make—making choices and entering the life of the retirement community since her massive task of caring is completed.

I see other couples contending with one partner's suffering from some form of dementia. Some are able make this work by having respite care person for the person with this disability for a time or two a week. Others are able to provide supportive care with their partner residing in the memory care unit, and they can be present, visit, help with that extra service provided.

### Joseph and Myra

Meika Loe tells of a couple she met in her study of older adults. Joseph and Myra are holocaust survivors. A barber by profession, he once escaped being executed by offering to cut the comandante's hair. Though of modest means, they contribute as much as they can to cherished Jewish causes.

Age means nothing to me,
I can't get old.
I'm working.
I was old when I was twenty-one
And out of work. As long as you
Are working, you stay young.
When I am in front of an audience
And all that love and vitality sweeps
   over me
I forget my age

—George Burns

Meika observes, "Joseph and Myra live together in a small one-bedroom apartment. He is mostly blind, and she has severe dementia. He says, 'We are together; she is my eyes, and I am her memory.'"[5]

## CARING FOR ONE'S OWN AND
## OTHER GRANDCHILDREN

This part of my impressions starts far away but also comes near.

The country of Zimbabwe, like many low-income countries, lacks in resources to treat the mentally ill. A country of approximately 16.5 million people has approximately twelve psychiatrists.

One of those psychiatrists, Dr. Dixon Chibanda has been working to narrow this treatment gap. It began when one of his young patients could not afford the bus fare (about $15) to her appointment and instead hanged herself. In 2007, he set out to create an informal system of therapists for each of these isolated communities. He commented "It suddenly dawned on me that one of the most reliable resources we have in Africa is grandmothers."

And so, he created an organization called Friendship Bench. This organization now trains hundreds of Zimbabwean grandmothers in problem-solving therapy, role-playing, and behavior activation. These trained grandmothers provide therapy outside on "Friendship Benches." Dr. Chibanda notes that "Grandmothers are often best equipped to provide care because they listen and guide their charges toward a solution, unlike other members of the community who tend to direct their patients what to do."

This movement with its training and Friendship Benches has expanded to at least four other African Countries and has made its way to New York City and Davos, Switzerland. Chibanda says, "My dream is to take this to scale. With something simple, we make a difference in the world."[6]

With or without the "Friendship Bench" grandparents as a whole offer much care and healing to the world. When my first grandchild was born, an older woman told me, "Now you will discover what love really is." And she was right. Mary Pipher notes, "For the most part, grandparents are not about power, fame, money, or sex, but rather about love—perhaps the purist and least exploitable love—that humans can feel for one another."[7] Teachers tell her that they can tell which children have grandparents close by and interested in them. A teacher notes such children are "quieter, calmer, and more trusting."

Of course, this caring picture is not universal. Some grandparents feel they have raised their children and are finished with that. Others have small children thrust into their responsibility, because of problems of the child's parents—addiction or incarceration, perhaps. And, in this age of lower birth-rates, there are a good number of older people who long for grandchildren but will not have any.

Still for a great number, grandparenting is a lovely time of deep joy and caring. This may provide a clue for a religious leader learning how to relate to older adults. Ask about grandchildren. This may propel the conversation into enthusiastic stories and pictures, or for some it may not. As a bumper sticker playfully put it, "If I'd known how great my grandchildren are, I'd have had them first." We will return to this subject from another angle in chapter 9.

## FINDING A GIFT TO GIVE OTHERS

### George

An assisted living resident, George Garris told Beth Baker, "I didn't come here to die—I came to contribute something to somebody."[8] Such courage can be seen both in persons in retirement facilities and those still living independently.

### Marylee

Brent Walker, formerly director of a nonprofit agency advocating for religious freedom, recalls an elderly friend who was just such a person, "Marylee Sturgis was an unlikely fighter for religious liberty and church state separation," he wrote. His first impression "Elderly, unimposing, walking with some difficulty . . . with the help of a cane." However, a retired librarian, this frail appearance did not keep her sharp mind from discovering and discussing many topics of religious freedom around the world. In time, her curiosity and leadership led to her being appointed to the national board of the Baptist Joint Committee for Religious Liberty (BJC).

Brent recalls, "I'll always remember her first board meeting. I was a little concerned about how she—then in her late seventies and physically challenged, would travel from Charlottesville (Virginia) to Washington D.C." "No problem," Marylee said, "I'll drive." Alone? "Yes of course." And, he remembers, "She maneuvered her well-travelled boat-like car into the teeth of beltway traffic, finding her way to the hotel and meeting site in the heart of D.C.—and, without a GPS!"

When she died at the age of eighty-seven, it was revealed that "she put money to her words and deeds in death. Turns out, this frugal, simple-living retired University of Virginia librarian made the largest testamentary gift the BJC has ever received"—as well as gifts to other organizations whose causes she cherished.[9]

## A Quaker Woman

Parker Palmer tells of a similar encounter. To learn more about Quakers with whom he would be working, he went to a national gathering of that group. As he came in, he noticed several elderly women chatting with each other. "Each of them had her white hair tied up in a bun—the way my grandmother wore hers." He smiled and thought how nice it was to have memories of his grandmother rekindled.

However, in the midst of this reverie, one of the women walked up to him. He recalls, "Without any preliminaries, she grabbed my arm as if to keep me from fleeing, and said, 'I've just returned from a meeting in Des Moines about Native American rights, and I want to tell you what I learned.'" She proceeded to do this and attempted to recruit him for her project. Palmer concluded, "She's not Grandma and apple pie! She's the kind of person I want to be when I'm an old man!"[10]

## Bill

Sometimes, the expression of care can be to one lonely person. For several years, Bill Buffet has been corresponding with a person in prison for life. This is through the PEN America program, an organization that matches writers with prisoners interested in writing.

He writes, shares, and listens to his prisoner friend, a transgender person named Steve, but who prefers the name "Kat." Kat tells him of the frustrating struggle to get the hormone treatments to which she is legally entitled. She also writes and gives progress reports of her care for an injured baby sparrow, that survived and thrived under her tender care for a while but eventually died.

Now Kat can also call him. Through an organization called jPay, Bill sends a modest amount of money each month, which Kat can deposit and then be allowed to have a fifteen-minute conversation, unless something snafus.

Bill is eighty-five and Kat is sixty-six, and he intends they will be in touch for as long as they can. As he asks what this means, Bill reflects, "I've never been interested in the question, 'What is the meaning of life?' but I know that Kat gives meaning to mine. We are important to each other. We enjoy each other's letters and our phone calls. She reminds me to never take anything in my life for granted. My life is one of privilege and I must never forget.

I hope I'm a reminder for Kat that life exists beyond the wretched walls that confine her. And that someone—beyond the razor wire, alarms, and steel doors—cares and is listening."[11]

## Dusty

I also remember a much-loved church member, Dusty. As my colleague Ruth Rosell recalls, "Dusty went through significant trials in later life. However, what he did was find meaning in his hospital room. He was an other-centered person, and he got to know all the caregivers. He really connected with all the people who went through his room. When the caregiver was from another country, he asked about that country. He was trying to get these staff persons to teach him Spanish. He was with people right where he was." And he continued being that kind of person right up to the day he died.

## Ray

A while back, I received one of these acts of caring. A few months ago, I went to the dining hall to eat and found a place to sit at a table with "Dutch" and "Ray." Dutch is a World War II veteran who was injured in service, and Ray struggles with Parkinson's Disease. They had already been served. Even though the wait staff is usually efficient, that day I could not seem to get a waiter's attention, and I was in a hurry (I no longer remember why). Ray lifted his plate and said something I didn't understand. I asked him to repeat it—with shaking hands he again lifted his plate to offer me the second half of his sandwich. I accepted it and ate it—it felt more like holy communion. I left without attention from a waiter, having been served by Ray. Not long after that, Ray had to be transferred to assisted living.

## Maxine

I think also of Maxine, a retired teacher. Early in her retirement, she took the Stephen Ministry training (a yearlong course in caring-listening skills) at her church. In addition to outreach among church members, she was asked to be a volunteer chaplain in the huge University Hospital nearby. At that time, the hospital had only one employed chaplain. And so, she responded. Maxine went twice a week and spent five hours each time reaching out to patients. She recalls, "I started when I was seventy and walked those long halls for sixteen years. Basically, I just listened and prayed for patients. It was so rewarding, and I hated to give it up." When she could no longer do all that walking, she accepted an invitation to be a greeter in the waiting room for radiation Oncology patients and their families. Only when her husband Ross fell and suffered a cracked femur, did she have to give that up as well.

## PROFILES IN CREATIVITY

Recently, the retirement community where I live had "An Artful Evening Gallery Night." Persons were invited to display their arts and crafts. Twenty-five residents and seven staff persons brought their work. It was so enjoyable to see the wide variety of art that various residents provided, most of whom I did not know had such talents. There were quilts and other fabric art. There was a variety of wooden bowls, carved on a lathe. There were a few of the kites one resident makes as his hobby. There were beautiful and varied pictures from a variety of different media. It was an evening of celebration and wonder, of recognizing talents and gifts in each other that we did not know existed.

### Ellen

And that show by no means exhausted all the creativity among us. I think of Ellen, our near neighbor. Ellen has macular degeneration and cannot see a person five feet away from her. However, she somehow can still see up close well enough to thread a needle and creates the most exquisite needlepoint works of art, some of them huge. One of hers is a large bouquet of flowers that appears to be a vivid painting until coming within a few feet of it. She has also needlepoint large, vibrant, and jolly Santas, her favorites.

### Gloria and Other Musicians

Gloria has been a piano teacher all her life as was her mother before her. She plays and accompanies others beautifully. People accompanied by her can expect, careful and precise preparation and performance. She brought her piano with her to her retirement apartment and still provides lessons with a few people. During the stay at home orders she and her three young students learned how to do their piano lessons on "Face Time." There are also a number of us who sing in community choruses or church choirs, and some of us still play in community bands and other ensembles.

### Creativity Outside

When spring comes, much creativity goes outside. Many are busy in their small garden plots, some above ground, and others in the ground. Some gardens are totally food bearing. Others combine practical crops with a touch of beauty around the edges. One woman creates a flower garden that thrives, changes, and grows throughout the summer rivaling the beauty of the professional landscaping nearby that the staff members provide.

Another couple brought their experience with bluebirds. They proposed putting up bluebird houses to the residents' council, and it was approved. With guidance from the local Bluebird Association, a half dozen of the proper style and size birdhouses have been strategically placed—100 yards apart. Bird watchers eagerly await the spring migration, hoping some blue birds will take advantage of this and make their homes among us.

## AND SO

Does all this seem rather mundane and commonplace to you? Then I invite you to reconsider. Suppose you came on a first visit to our community. While you may have thought our facilities are nice, as you look at us residents you might be unimpressed. Our median age is somewhere in the eighties. We are wrinkled, gray haired or bald, stooped, perhaps a third of us using walkers, some more on canes, and a couple dozen in wheelchairs. But then you open your eyes, ears, and heart, and you see all the thriving, caring, creating that we are doing despite our infirmities. I hope that would spark your interest, broaden your vision, and increase your respect. Then, perhaps, you will be ready to minister among us.

## FOR REFLECTING AND CONVERSING

1. What memories did the stories in this chapter stir for you? Whose story, if any, touched you the most?
2. What contributions are older adults making to your faith community or agency?
3. Who is the most unique, or the most interesting, or the most talented older adult you have ever met?
4. How do the stories in this chapter enrich your approach and conversation as you meet and minister with older adults?
5. What thoughts, brainstorms, or implications for your ministry with older adults came to you from the persons you met in this chapter?

## NOTES

1. Matthew Cole Weiss, "20 People Who Did Great Things after 50," accessed March 27, 2020, https://www.ranker.com/list/accomplishments-after-50/matthew coleweiss.

2. Aronson, *Elderhood*, 348.

3. Elizabeth MacKinlay, *Spiritual Growth and Care in The Fourth Age of Life* (London and Philadelphia: Jessica Kingsley Publishers, 2006), 172.

4. David Schneider, *Arrows of Light: Devotions for Worldwide Christians* (Kearney, NE: Morris Publishing, 2006).

5. Meika Loe, *Aging Our Way: Lessons for Living from 85 and Beyond* (New York: Oxford, 2011), 170.

6. Evan Shapiro, "A Humble Solution to Global Depression," *Time*, February 18–25, 2019, 30.

7. Pipher, *Another Country*, 276–77.

8. Beth Baker, *Old Age in a New Age: The Promise of Transformative Nursing Homes* (Nashville: Vanderbilt University Press, 2007), 39.

9. Brent Walker, e mail 10/20/2018.

10. Parker Palmer, *On the Brink of Everything: Grace, Gravity, and Getting Old* (Oakland: Berrett-Kohler, 2018), 115–16.

11. Bill Buffet, "#026260 A Prisoner's Story, Continued," *Baptist Peacemaker*, July–September 38, no. 3 (2018): 5–8.

# Chapter 4

# Laugh and Play with Us

A cheerful heart is good medicine, but a downcast spirit dries up the bones.

— Proverbs 17:22

When the LORD restored the fortunes of Zion, . . . our mouth was filled with laughter, and our tongue with shouts of joy.

—Psalm 126,1-2

Common sense and a sense of humor are the same thing, moving at different speeds.

—William James[1]

The other day I was sitting in a lounge outside the little grocery store at the retirement community where I live. I was waiting for the salads to be delivered. There was another person there, a woman with flowing gray hair. She was in her wheelchair. We started chatting and I told her what I was waiting for. She said she was waiting for her appointment in the beauty salon and continued, "I'm going to get a haircut, so I won't look like an English sheepdog." We had a chuckle at that. Shortly after that the salads arrived, and we went to our separate errands.

Throughout the day, each time I thought of her words, I found myself chuckling again. I enjoyed talking with this person so comfortable with herself that she could playfully "worry" about looking like an English sheep dog!

# HAPPINESS AND CONTENTMENT
## AMONG OLDER ADULTS

Why do I tell you this little experience, and what does it have to do with our ministries with older adults? Two reasons. For one, it points to the truth that, on the whole, older adults are much more content and happier than society at large imagines. Indeed, on average, they are happier than persons in other life stages.

A number of studies have discovered and established this truth. The University of Warwick interviewed two million people from eighty nations, and this revealed an extraordinarily consistent response. Whatever the nation, whether rich or poor, fertile or without children, married or single, people were unhappiest in middle age and happiest when children or older adults.[2]

A recent investigation also supports this finding. In reporting on this study, Deborah Netburn notes, "Believe it or not, there are upsides to getting older." Though physical health may decline with age, "research suggests that your overall mental health, including your mood, your sense of well-being and your ability to handle stress keeps improving right up until the very end of life."[3]

She is reporting the findings of a research project that contacted 1,500 San Diego residents aged 21 to 99 and learned that "people in their 20s were the most stressed out and depressed, while those in their 90s were the most content." Dilip Jeste, senior author of the study noted, "The consistency was really striking. People who were in older life were happier, more satisfied, less depressed, had less anxiety and less perceived stress than younger respondents."

Laura Carstensen, director of the Stanford Center on Longevity, commented "In the literature it's called the paradox of aging," but it is not really a paradox at all. "When people face endings, they tend to shift from goals about exploration and expanding horizons to ones about savoring relationships and focusing on meaningful activities" and so "life gets better, you feel better, and the negative emotions become less frequent and more fleeting when they occur."

The San Diego study did not include persons who had dementia, lived in a nursing home, or had a terminal illness. And so, the elders in the survey were probably overall fairly healthy.[4]

I tested this out with a group of older adults in my community. I asked these folks, mostly in their eighties, "When were you the happiest and most content? At 21? At 51? Or Now?" By show of hands, 1 chose "21," 5 chose "51," and 15 chose "now."

Another pair of researchers have taken this a step further. They have gone on from general well-being to a study of playfulness among older adults.

Indeed, Careen Yarnal and Xinyi Qian could find no studies on older-adult playfulness, noting that most of the research on older Americans is negative or disease oriented. By contrast, they assert "Playfulness . . . holds great potential for contributing to healthy aging." Further, they "postulate that adult playfulness might be an important characteristic of cognitive functioning and emotional growth, both components of healthy aging."[5] And so they set out to create an Older-Adult Playfulness scale.

They went through carefully focused data gathering, designing and testing the validity of their OAP, *Older-Adult Playfulness* inventory. Their conclusion is that there are four factors that include fifteen identifiable qualities in their OAP:

Factor one is that "playful older adults are psychologically upbeat: they are happy, optimistic, cheerful, joyful, relaxed and enthused individuals." There is a combination of high arousal, low arousal, and generic qualities.

Factor two is that "playful older adults are behaviorally impish: they act in mischievous, naughty, clowning, and teasing ways." This does not need to be marked by physically rigorous activities that were part of childhood, adolescent, or younger adult playfulness. Further, older adults seem to learn how to embody these qualities without being disruptive as younger persons might be.

Factor three is that "playful older adults are cognitively spontaneous: they are creative and whimsical. . . . older adults take playfulness a step further. Playful older adults are primed to initiate something novel, unexpected, or quirky." This leads them to note "playfulness is more than a trait. It is 'an attitude of throwing off constraint.'"

And factor 4 is that "playful adults are amusing; they are observably funny and humorous, which, in turn, solicits positive responses from others."[6]

These scholars have done some important work. They are to be appreciated for focusing on older adults, discovering our uniqueness in being playful, and opening the door to further appreciative research.

At the same time, their description of our playfulness raises a couple of questions. For one, are we playful older adults if we lack a number of these qualities, but are drawn to those who possess them in fuller measure? I remember a truly Playful Older Adult, Donna Beth. She had been confined to a wheelchair with Parkinson's for many years, yet she never lost her playful, iconoclastic, and often sarcastic sense of humor. When she came to a meal function, many of us would be there early, hoping to get a place at her table. There would be laughter throughout the evening, both initiated by Donna Beth, and by what she stirred in the others of us. At the end of the evening, we would long for the playful repartee to go on and on.

My question is this: Are those of us who lack Donna Beth's gifts but admire, enjoy, and enter into them also playful older adults?

My second question is this: How does that inventory relate to us introverts doing introvert types of things? Of course, introvert does not describe whether a person is gifted relationally or not; introvert simply indicates where a person is renewed and gets energy. For introverts, this energy renewal may come from a solitary activity or time with one person or a very few close friends.

For example, when I find a great novel, I (an introvert) can spend an entire afternoon and evening deeply absorbed in it. I regret the need to interrupt it for food and sleep. The world of the novelist becomes real to me, I connect with the characters and am eager to see what happens next to them.

This leads me to wonder, do the qualities these researchers identify refer more to extroverts and extrovert activities? How would an introvert be seen? As I raise this question, I am answering for myself. I claim the next novel I find and my encounter it with great fun and an invitation to enter another world for a while.

Further, what about the introvert activity of creative writing or other solitary artistic activities? I conclude that some of us are playful introverts even if other personality types—and the new inventory—may find that hard to recognize.

## HUMOR AMONG OLDER ADULTS

The second reason for telling the "English sheep dog" story is that it provides a window not only into the contentment and happiness of older adults. It also points to our humor, jokes, and storytelling. To frame this exploration, consider some reflection on humor in general. Then we will explore how older adults engage these possibilities.

There are so many kinds of humor, of course—teasing, wisecracks, word play, limericks, anecdotes, pretend insults, jokes, riddles, and puns, to name just a few. Then there are sight gags, pranks, physical humor, and playful toys (rubber noses and more).

Out of all these possible varieties, Peter Berger offered a helpful typology of humor in his book *Redeeming Laughter: The Comic Dimension of Human Experience*.[7] He speaks about four different genres or forms of expression of the comic and what each uniquely does.

One type he mentions is *benign humor*—the comic as diversion. This is the simplest, most common type of humor. It is the stuff of children's play with their frequent giggles and laughter at little unexpected things. "Benign humor . . . is harmless, even innocent. It is intended to evoke pleasure, relaxation, and good will. It enhances rather than disrupts the flow of everyday life."[8] This kind of humor provides a brief vacation from our worries so we can return refreshed and ready for whatever life gives us. Laughing at ourselves is a frequent and lovely form of benign humor.

Another of Berger's types of humor is *tragicomedy*—humor as consolation. This form may be described as laughter through tears. "Tragicomedy . . . is mellow, forgiving. It does not bring about a profound catharsis, but it is moving, nonetheless. Above all else, it consoles. . . [T]he tragic is not banished, not defied, not absorbed. It is, as it were, momentarily suspended."[9]

Still another type of humor is *wit*. This is engaging humor as an intellectual game. In wit the comic uses humor to gain insight and express reality that might be otherwise missed. It is the use of intelligence and thought functions in humor. Granted that all humor uses intellect, in this form the intellect is more prominent and may be the only purpose of the exercise. How the humor might affect others is a lesser consideration. Jokes, epigrams, puns all may be ways that wit is expressed.[10]

Berger notes one other type of humor, satire—"the deliberate use of the comic for purposes of attack."[11] The attack may be against institutions and their representatives. Or it may be directed at other groups of people or be at an individual such as a political opponent.

There are nuances of this type of humor. For example, the use of irony may also attack something, but usually with a little more tolerance of human frailty and weakness. And parody may also confront but with more playfulness.

These humor types offer an insight into older-adult humor-playfulness. I believe we older persons have learned how to combine all four of these types, or at least the first three—self-humor, tragicomedy, and wit into a way of living. It is often said that if you do not laugh at your pains and problems, you won't have much to laugh about. And so, we do. We sometimes joke about these difficulties with a twinkle in our eyes and a chuckle in our throats.

> Comedy bears within it a great secret. This secret is the promise of redemption. For redemption promised in eternity is what comedy gives us in its few moments of precarious liberation—the collapse of the walls of our imprisonment.
>
> —Peter Berger

## DO YOU WANT SOME EXAMPLES?[12]

We joke about our aches and pains. In a cartoon, one older woman speaks to another, "Even when I'm naked, I wish I could slip into something comfortable." Another older person relates "I feel like my body has gotten out of shape, so I got my doctor's permission to join a fitness club. I decided to take an aerobics class for seniors. I bent, twisted, gyrated, jumped up and down, and perspired for an hour. But by the time I got my leotards on, the class was over."

We joke about health issues. One of my favorite humorists, Dave Downs, a fellow resident where I live, recently demonstrated this kind of humor. He had been suffering fainting spells, and tests revealed that he needed a heart pacemaker. Before surgery, he wrote a limerick for his cardiologist.

I don't have the patience to bicker
My heart rate's reduced to a flicker
      When it acts up this way,
      I faint dead away
Please fix up my troublesome ticker.
      After his successful surgery and installing of a pacemaker,
  one his friends, Don Liebenberg wrote him.
I'm glad you fixed up your ticker
      Before you got any sicker
          Know that our thoughts
          Are with you and auts
      And your ticker will tick without flicker.
      And so, Dave answered him—
      I once had a troublesome ticker
      The danged thing went quicker and quicker.
          My pacer kicks in,
          To slow it again,
      I now have no cause to be sicker.
          In turn, Don replied,
      Thank heaven you have a good pacer
      To steady your ticker, a racer
      The times you have spent
      Running hell bent
      You now have no need to go chase her
          To which Dave responded,
      You seem to think I should chase her
      But I wouldn't wish to abase her
      Because of our ages
      We're thought of as sages.
      Like pencils, I'm scared I'd eraser.[13]

Believe it or not, the exchange continues from there, but we will go on without them.

We joke about our sagging bodies. Two older women read about "streaking" and decided to do it. They took off their clothes and walked briskly around the grounds of their retirement community. Two older men, sitting on a bench, saw them go by. "What's that?" one asked. The other replied, "I don't know, but it needs ironing."

We joke about our body functions. An older woman walks into a bar and orders a scotch with two drops of water. She orders a second and a third. Finally, the bartender asks her, "What's with the two drops of water?" She answers, "Well, young man, I'll tell you, when you get to be my age, you know how to hold your scotch, but your water is another matter."[14]

We joke about our changing experience of sexuality. An old man was sitting on a riverbank fishing when he heard, "Help! Help!" He looked down and saw a frog. The frog said, "Kiss me and I will become a beautiful princess." The man picked up the frog and put it in his pocket. "Aren't you going to kiss me?" the frog asked. He answered, "At my age, I'd rather have a talking frog."

On a man's ninetieth birthday party, his buddies had arranged for one of those huge birthday cakes with a "surprise" inside. As the party guests sang to him, a beautiful scantily dressed woman jumped out of the cake and told the "birthday boy," "I can offer you super sex!" He thought a moment and replied, "I guess I'll take the soup."

We joke about our memory issues. One old fellow had not seen his buddy for a few days but saw him sitting on his front porch. "Where have you been?" "We've been doctoring. I've gone to a memory doctor and he gave me some new pills." "Are they helping?" "Oh yes, my memory is much better now." "I might go see that doctor and get some of those pills. What's the doctor's name?" The old fellow paused for a moment and said, "Those pretty red flowers with thorns, what are they called?" "Roses." "Oh yeah, Rose, what is the name of my new doctor?"

Then there is the "Senility Prayer," a takeoff on the "Serenity Prayer," "Grant me the senility to forget the people I never liked anyway, the good fortune to run into the ones I do, and the eyesight to tell the difference."

Sometimes, we even joke about death. An elderly woman decided to prepare her will and came to tell her pastor about two requests. "First, I want to be cremated. Second, I want my ashes spread at Walmart." "Why Walmart?" the pastor asked. "Then I'll be sure my daughters visit me twice a week."

And here is one of the most powerful stories of tragicomedy I have ever read: Paul Stevens recalls his friend Brian Smith who was slowly deteriorating and dying from ALS—the "Lou Gehrig disease." When he lost the ability to swallow, his health providers inserted a gastric feeding tube. After a couple of days, he had composed the "Top Ten Advantages to Having a G Tube," and listed them in David Letterman style:

No. 10 You can brush your teeth while you eat.
No. 9 You can drink all you want and still be able to
    say "alcohol has never touched my lips."

No. 8 You can eat Brussels sprouts and never have to smell them.

No. 7 You can eat at McDonald's and never have to taste the food.

No. 6 You have twice the belly button lint.

No. 5 You can talk with your bag full.

No. 4 You can eat at Hooters and the waitresses stare at you!

No. 3 You never have to complain that the food isn't hot enough.

No. 2 It gives the term "body piercing" a whole new meaning.

No. 1 When you wash out the system you get to drink your own dish water.[15]

A gastric feeding tube is no joking matter, and yet Brian Smith coura-geously dealt with it that way. He is no longer alive, and yet this humor touches and inspires me every time I read it.

## HUMOR AND YOUR MINISTRY AMONG US

How does one engage these insights about humor and play in ministry with older adults? For starters, be open, be aware. We might not get your humor. It may come from a different time and experiences than ours.

You may not recognize our humor, either. As a younger pastor, I now see where I missed or misunderstood elder humor at times. Early in one pastorate, there was an (elderly) men's prayer breakfast on Saturday mornings. I tried to come some of the time, even though it lengthened an already busy day for me. One member, Harold always had a comment for me, "Oh, did you finally decide to come? . . . Is your watch broke? . . . Didn't you know when we meet? Etc." I concluded that Harold didn't like me.

Only later did I realize that Harold said those things *because* he liked me. He was that way with all his friends. Playful insults are a part of some older males' humor. If you hear a man greet another with "Jack, you old horse thief. You're getting uglier all the time," you can know they are particularly good long-term friends!

Another time, a woman long confined to a wheelchair once greeted me, "Why hello pastor, I'd love to get up and make you a cup of tea." I was slow to recognize the courageous self-humor—tragicomedy with which she spoke. She was also reminding me "Don't define me by my handicap."

The comedians we enjoy may vary from generation to generation. I asked a group of older adults who were their favorite comedians. Their answer— Will Rogers Bob Hope, Jack Benny, George Burns and Gracie Allen, Fibber Magee and Molly, Carol Burnett, Tim Conway, Harvey Corman, Bob Newhart, Smothers Brothers, Abbot and Costello, Don Rickles, Monty Python, and one new comedian, Bill Maher.

So come, open to relaxing, enjoying, entering our sometimes playful, jok-ing, teasing world. Be quicker than I was to discover that if the joke is on you, you are being accepted.

One other caution. Be aware that jokes about aging sound different when coming from a younger person. They are no longer "self-humor," and they may feel more like a put down than tragicomedy. Tell stories about yourself and your life stage. (That is, if people in your life stage laugh at themselves.) And if you tell jokes about old people to old people, make sure that first we know you love us!

Do males and females experience and express humor differently? Out of her studies with eighty-five-year-old plus people, Meika Loe observed that the older adult men told more jokes, while women told her that joking was not part of their lives. Still she found the women "used wit or delighted in telling humorous stories and laughed readily during interviews."[16] Both kinds of humor are worthy and to be appreciated.

There is a fair amount of humor that goes on in the conflicts between the sexes. I once saw a woman, whose t-shirt on the front said, "Women must do twice as much as men to succeed." The back said, "Fortunately, it's not that difficult."

This is another opportunity to draw closer to older adults and possibly find some ministry opportunities. In addition to specific humor, explore older adults play and playfulness. Learn about the hobbies, crafts, and activities we enjoy. It may be good to ask, what do you enjoy doing now? Also ask, what did you used to love to do but do not (or cannot) do anymore?

You may discover a wider world of play and playfulness than you expected. At the retirement community where I live, there are

- Weekly game groups—bridge, euchre, Wii bowling, Mah Jong, dominoes. Tripoli,
- Exercise groups for various levels of strength and agility, including Tai Chi, chair yoga, music in motion, warm water exercise, balance enhancing exercise, circuit walks, hand weights, fluff tennis,
- Activity and discussion groups including various Bible studies, watercolor, "Turning Points in American History," "The Hubble Telescope," "Forensic Science," memoir writing, book club, quilting group,
- Attending arts events (with bus transportation provided) to symphony, concert band, dinner theatre, nature outings, Civil War band reenactment, and more.
- In process jigsaw puzzles in several places where anyone can stop by and add a piece or two.
- At Halloween, a hilarious and creative pumpkin decorating contest.
- Garden plots, both in and above ground for any who want to take part and a handy man's club that shares a workshop, activities, and projects.
- Informal spontaneous groups. For example, three of us who play baritone horns found each other, get together to play, and are occasionally asked to play for a community event.

When Roland Martinsen interviewed a number of older adults varying in age from their sixties to nineties, he noted,

"These elders laugh, crack jokes, travel, play tennis, golf, walk, hike, canoe, sing, play instruments, restore old tractors, pose for sexy-old-ladies calendars, go for the best body of the year, read, write parodies, make videos, throw parties, host movie nights and simple conversations, rest, and relax."

As he reflects on what he has seen and heard in these interviews, he muses, "If old age is supposed to be a mostly sad, ever serious isolated existence, it most certainly is not so among these elders. There is liveliness, levity, frivolity, laughter, lightheartedness and much just plain fun."[17]

## WHAT AND HOW CAN THIS MINISTRY OF HUMOR HAPPEN?

If your ministry is with scattered or isolated older adults, it may be more difficult for the people in your care to be a part of the play and enjoyment activities as they would like.

It may be good to inquire with questions like, what would you like to do for enjoyment? What is keeping you from it? Their answers might reveal opportunities for a ministry of play.

My hunch is that often what is keeping people from the playful activities they would enjoy, is transportation, or lack of it. Even the older adults who are driving may not drive at night anymore.

In one of my pastorates, we happened on a popular but very simple activity. My family and I had enjoyed going to a free outdoor symphony concert in a city park, about an hour from where we lived. We thought how much others might enjoy this, and so we announced the date of the next concert and said we would take as many as our two church vans could hold to that concert and back. Mostly older adults signed up, and we nearly filled both vans. An evening of beautiful music under the stars, with pleasant company going up and coming back. It was so enjoyed that we repeated it several times.

At another time, my wife Mary Ann invited two women in their nineties to go with us to our local art museum's special display on native American art. We picked them up at their homes, set the pace to fit their needs, took them to lunch in the lovely museum cafeteria. They so enjoyed and were so grateful for an experience they could not have had without Mary Ann's thoughtfulness.

In another church, someone came up with the idea of an intergenerational bridge group. She put out a public invitation to anyone who would like to join in, part of the church or not, whatever age, whatever level of skill. A warm, playful monthly bridge gathering came into being. My wife and I joined in as long as we were there.

In this chapter, I have been attempting two quite simple things which may have great significance for your ministry. I have asked you to recognize the basic happiness, contentment, joy that is found in many older people. Then I have encouraged you to discover their humor and play, enter into it, and if possible, expand their opportunities for it. This may be not only enjoyable in itself; it may open the door to deeper relationships and ministry. For, as Victor Borge once said, "Laughter is the shortest distance between two people."

On a lovely summer evening, a busload of us in our retirement community went to hear a performance by an outstanding concert band. They had offered a wide variety of music from many periods of history. One selection that evening was "Alice Blue Gown." That must have touched a tender memory for one of the women in our group. As we rode back in the darkened bus, she could be heard quietly singing or humming "Alice Blue Gown" over and over again all the way back. It was a perfect benediction on a beautiful evening. A busload of older adults were having a more playful and joyous evening than outsiders might have imagined possible.

## FOR REFLECTING AND CONVERSING

1. What memories or "aha's" did this chapter stir in you?
2. What, if anything, surprised you in this chapter?
3. What are you doing well in recognizing and facilitating older adults' humor, laughter, and play?
4. What opportunities occurred to you as you read this chapter? How might these possibilities enhance your relationships or broaden your ministry with older adults?
5. The chapter has mentioned some nuances and cautions about humor with older adults. What questions or cautions do you have about humor-play with older adults?

## NOTES

1. Quoted in Palmer, *On the Brink of Everything*, 80.
2. Ashton Applewhite, *This Chair Rocks: A Manifesto Against Ageism* (Networked Books, 2016), 49–50. She is summarizing University of Warwick, "Middle-Aged Misery Spans the Globe," *Science Daily*, January 30, 2008, http://www.sciencedaily.com/releases/2008/01/08129080710.htm.

3. Deborah Netburn, "The Aging Paradox: The Older We Get, The Happier We Are," accessed September 28, 2019, https://www.psychiatrist.com/jcp/article/pages/2016/v77n08/v77n0813.aspx. The quotes in the following two paragraphs are from this source.

4. Netburn, "The Aging Paradox."

5. Careen Yarnal and Xinyi Qian, "Older-Adult Playfulness: An Innovative Construct and Measurement for Healthy Aging Research," *American Journal of Play* 4, no. 1 (Summer 2011): 53.

6. Yarnal and Qian, "Older Adult Playfulness," 72–73.

7. Peter L. Berger, *Redeeming Laughter: The Comic Dimension of Human Experience* (New York: Walter De Gruyter), 1997.

8. Berger, *Redeeming Laughter*, 108.

9. Berger, *Redeeming Laughter*, 117.

10. Berger, *Redeeming Laughter*, 139.

11. Berger, *Redeeming Laughter*, 157–58.

12. Except where explicitly acknowledged, these pieces of humor are widely spread among older people, on forwarded emails, conversations, and more.

13. David Downs, personal correspondence, used with permission.

14. Loe, *Aging Our Way*, 151.

15. Brian Smith, Closing *Comments: ALS—a Spiritual Journey into the Heart of a Fatal Affliction* (Jacksonville Beach, FL: Clements Publishing, 2000) 90, quoted in R. Paul Stevens, *Aging Matters: Finding your calling for the rest of your life* (Grand Rapids: William B. Eerdman's, 2016), 148.

16. Loe, *Aging Our Way*, 148.

17. Martenson, *Elders Rising*, 166.

# Reflections of a Marvelous Spirit

## ON THE SUBJECT OF AGING

At eighty-six, Rosie and I live by the rules of the elderly. If the toothbrush is wet, you have cleaned your teeth. If the bedside radio is warm in the morning, you left it on all night. If you are wearing one brown and one black shoe, quite probably you have a like pair in the closet.

Rosie has aged some in the past year, and now seems like a woman entering her forties. She deplores with me, the miscreant who regularly enters our house in the middle of the night, squeezes the toothpaste tube in the middle and departs.

As for me, I am about as bright as can be expected, remembering the friend who told me years ago, "If your I.Q. ever breaks 100, sell!"

Like most elderly people, we spend happy hours in front of our TV set. We rarely turn it on, of course.

I walk with a slight straddle, hoping people will think I just got off a horse. I considered carrying a riding crop but gave it up—too ostentatious.

I stagger when I walk and small boys follow me, making bets on which way I'll go next. This upsets me; children shouldn't gamble.

On my daily excursions, I greet everyone punctiliously, including the headrests in parked, empty cars. Dignified friends seem surprised when I salute them with a breezy "Hi!" They don't realize I haven't enough breath for some huge two-syllable word of greeting.

My motto this year is from the Spanish: "I don't want the cheese, I just want to get out of this trap."

When we are old, the young are kinder to us, and we are kinder to each other. There is a sunset glow that irradiates our faces and is reflected in the faces of those around us. But it is still sunset.

The late Bruce Bliven

From Richard Bolles, *The Three Boxes of Life and How to Get Out of Them*, copyright © 1978, 1981, p. 351 Used by permission of Ten Speed Press, an imprint of Random House, a division of Penguin Random House LLC. All rights reserved.

## Chapter 5

# Hear and Respond

## *Our Housing and Work Questions*

Do not cast me off in the time of old age; do not forsake me when my strength is spent.

—Psalm 71:9

So far in this book, I have wanted to convince you that there is a new older adult population—more vigorous, creative, living longer, and larger in numbers than any previous time in human history. This older population has interesting and admirable persons within it, many of them playful, and some downright humorous. There are older persons who are visionary and dedicated to advancing various causes. There are opportunities for vital ministry with these fascinating and lively older adults.

Now the focus changes. These older adults also come to times of hardship and difficulty. In the next two chapters, we will consider several of the changes, decisions, and frailties in the older years. In this chapter, I will discuss employment-income and housing-location decisions. In the next, the topic will be the many health issues and chronic diseases that can pop up on the aging journey. These are some of the places where we may need your help.

In this chapter and next, I have asked my friend Dr. Jon Dedon to contribute out of his professional experience. He is a geriatrician and teaches in the University of Missouri, Kansas City, Medical School. In his practice, he has had wide experience with frail older adults who need 24/7 care. He will describe the choices and experience for older adults in that time of life.

A religious leader is wise to be to know about these issues and be aware when persons are facing one or more of them. It is also important to be aware of resource people and agencies that can help and guide. Such resource people may be among the older adults themselves, guiding others on roads they have already walked.

## HOW LONG TO WORK, AT WHAT, AND WHY?

One issue is the question how long will a person work? When will they retire? Some occupations—persons in the military forces, police, and firepersons for example—have a mandatory retirement age, somewhat younger than for many others. Others work in positions in which retirement compensation is set after a given number of years of work. Since benefits do not increase by working beyond that, they may elect to retire at that age. Still others may need to work past the traditional sixty-five-year retirement time in order to qualify for full social security benefits.

On the other hand, a recent poll revealed that one in four Americans has no plans to retire. This may be out of love for what one is doing, or out of financial need. Perhaps neither the employer nor the worker has provided sufficient funds to live on in retirement, so one hopes to be able to keep on working and drawing a salary. Many also have financial uncertainties about whether they will have the funds to pay for whatever health and care issues may arise in aging.

However, this plan to stay employed may not be realistic. A survey revealed that 26 percent of seniors who retired earlier than planned did so because they lost their jobs. Finding new jobs is slower and more difficult for the older worker. A Boston College study reported that workers 55 and over, spent 40.6 weeks unemployed (following the 2008–2009 recession) compared to 31.6 weeks of out of a job for the younger worker. New jobs late in one's career are less likely to have the level of pay and benefits of previous employment.[1]

Retired persons may find ways (occasional or short-term) to offer the benefits of their experience. For example, Ann, a retired Spanish teacher provides a tutoring service (immensely popular toward the end of semesters) and serves as a translator when needed in educational or medical settings. Carl, a retired school administrator might be called when a principal has to be absent for days, weeks, or months, to fill in providing leadership until the principal can return.

Changes in the needs of society may cause retired persons to return to work. During the COVID-19 pandemic, in several parts of the country, there was a request for retired health

> To know how to grow old is the masterwork of wisdom and one of the most difficult chapters in the great art of living.
>
> —Henri Frederic Amiel

care workers—including nurses, doctors, respiration therapists to return to work at least temporarily.

Some explore and enter "encore careers" in retirement. This may be continuation of some aspect of one's working career, or something quite new and different. I am one who had a delightful experience of this type—for nineteen years after retiring from being a pastor, I was a professor in a small seminary, teaching both out of my academic credentials and my years of experience in ministry. It was a lighter responsibility than being a pastor, and I loved the students, my colleagues, and the subjects I taught. Since I was on social security and a pension, I was able to do this for modest compensation that my employer could afford. Others may need to focus on the pay more than I did.

Often, the decisions people make about work as older adults reflect their financial situation. Some are living on the margin. Max Skidmore points out that 32 percent of older Americans derive at least 90 percent of their retirement income from their social security monthly income, and 20 percent of retirees have no other income than social security—about $16,000 a year. Retirees in this circumstance may find themselves having to choose between food and medications.[2]

## WHERE TO LIVE AND IN WHAT PLACE

Another area of decision has to do with where to live. There are two aspects of this question—what kind of housing-care arrangement and where geographically?

Throughout this discussion, I will illustrate by reflecting on two decision-making stories—that of Mary Ann and me and that of our friend Cynthia—"Cindy"—Haynes.

There are many older adults who want to stay in their home for many years. My wife and I faced the same issue. We had lived in the same house for more than thirty years. We loved the house, the yard, the neighborhood, the groups to which we belonged, and our many friends. We thought we were doing well in living there, caring for house and yard. Our family members saw more clearly that caring for our home was more physically taxing than we admitted, and in times of emergency, downright dangerous.

Further, we needed to evaluate whether the home we had enjoyed for thirty years would be suitable for aging in it. Would it be adequate through possible future emergencies? For example, is there a bedroom, a bathroom, and a kitchen on the same floor? (For us, no.) Is there easy access from outside? (no) Is there space in doorways, halls, and living areas for a walker or a wheelchair to move? (no) Then it was probably unwise to stay there.

Our friend Cindy was living with the same questions. After her husband Gordon died, she intended to stay in their home—the only home they had ever owned. She enjoyed its deck overlooking a large shaded back yard, a place for her to write in her journal, read, and pray. She appreciated being among people who had known them as a couple, both the people in her church and in her neighborhood.

However, a year or so later, while out walking, she slipped on a patch of mud and broke her right thumb. To her chagrin, they had to put it in a cast up to her elbow. For four or five months, her activity was restricted, and she depended on church and neighbor friends to drive and do errands for her. A year later, while struggling with a storm window that would not stay up, she had an accident that resulted in three compressed thoracic fractures in her vertebrae. This was both painful and inconvenient—she could not sleep in a bed or lie flat for about six months.

If that were not enough, an unusually wet year brought flooding to her basement—twice! Not only did these necessitate many repairs, it became clear that there she would have to have a diversion of water flow set up outside her house. By now it was clear, she could not stay and care for this home.

Liz O'Donnell notes, for some, there is the option to retrofit one's home. This may include "lowering shelves, removing any trip and fall hazards, lowering toilet seats, and widening doors to accommodate walkers and wheelchairs."[3] Or, for those who don't have that much money, take their chances in space that has some of these potential problems.

This is one possible answer to the question of housing—in our own home, equipped or not for what changes may be ahead. Many older adults strongly prefer this, argue for it, and may be willing to risk being alone when a fall or other emergency might happen. They may accept extra services—such as yard work, house cleaning, food or health needs—if it means they can stay in that home.

If or when the decision to move from the home of those previous years, there are two more decisions to consider: where, geographically, and what kind of housing-care facility should one choose?

An important part of the decision revolves around this question—who are the people who can and will help us as our needs grow greater and where are they? Family members often do these things, but in this day of much mobility, the potentially helpful family members are likely widespread. When I was pastor, from time to time, a beloved older member would need to tell us goodbye as they moved to be near a son or daughter who would provide the extra care needed.

Although Mary Ann and I resisted for a while, we knew that we needed to be nearer those who could help us with whatever our later older years might include. And so, in time, we moved some 400 miles from our home in suburban Kansas City to Madison, WI, where some family lived and worked.

As for Cindy's story, she also knew she needed to move out of her home, but where? She was grateful that her church was offering a discernment group, and so she entered in and processed her thoughts and feelings about moving. Should it be to a small apartment in the community where they had lived for so many years? If not that, where? She recalls, "The thought of leaving my beloved home, my green place, neighbors, and my church family, not to mention my burial plot next to Gordon made me very tearful."

Though friends had many suggestions about places to live nearby, in time it became clear. She needed to be near her two children and their families. Both of her children lived in the greater Houston, Texas area. And so, she, her family, and her support community worked to take the necessary steps—preparing the home for sale, disposing of what she would not need in a new place, and getting ready to go live in an area where she had never lived before. (I will continue her story shortly.)

The next question, both for Cindy and for us was this: If we know where we need to be geographically, what sort of housing and care arrangement should we choose there? There are a number of choices and a variety of costs.

Perhaps, what one can afford is smaller, simpler housing. They may find a small apartment, perhaps in subsidized senior housing, perhaps not. Friends who have gone into such settings with minimal services provided tell me that often the older adults themselves sometimes form support groups, game groups, and mutual care and support for each other.

There are other possibilities that have additional services and are more expensive. One is "Independent Living." This may be an apartment complex or cluster of cottages. Residents live independently but have access to a range of services such as dining rooms, activities, exercise programs, perhaps transportation to shopping, and entertainment events. This option offers a safe living space and an environment for social connections and friendships.

There are also continuous care retirement communities. As the name indicates, they have the range of all the levels that can respond to changing health and mobility needs. People might enter in the independent living portion, but have access to rehabilitation services, assisted living, or memory care when or if the need arises.

There are wide varieties in facilities, services, and amenities provided in such facilities. There is also a wide variety in the style and size of available housing. And there is variation in cost.

If the physical needs are greater, the choice might be "Assisted Living." Here there are additional services that can be negotiated/purchased. These might include assistance with tasks like bathing, dressing, housecleaning, laundry, and medication. While these facilities will have nursing staff, they are not designed to provide medical care or attention. Living in one of these facilities is not covered by Medicare or Medicaid.

If a person has memory issues, the facility needed might be a Memory Care Unit. These provide a high level of assisted living tasks, plus programming and recreational activities specifically designed for people with memory loss. These facilities almost always have a locked area, so residents will not wander or get lost.

With the assistance and advance scouting of our family members, Mary Ann and I eventually chose to live in the independent living part of a continuous care facility—It is a nonprofit, Lutheran sponsored retirement community. We selected a lovely apartment overlooking a community's "Green space."

The community into which Mary Ann and I moved speaks of the option to "age in place." That is, to continue to live in one's apartment but contract for services that may be needed. These may include nursing, cleaning, physical therapy, or other care activities. As a result, persons will be able to live in their own apartments for as long as possible.

Back to Cindy's story. Her immediate step was for she and her family to load a moving van with the household furnishings she would need, move it to Texas, and temporarily store it.

She then stayed with son David and family while she searched out her next living space. In her words, "I browsed through a number of facilities. I knew I wanted to be with other retired folk and get to know people. Not only was I concerned about prices, I also wanted to feel independent. Some apartment buildings were downtown and very tall. I knew I did not want to be in a hi-rise apt. I wanted to feel safe and able to walk outside."

"After all my research I only had to look at two places. God was so good. I found a place only—ten-to-fifteen-minute drive from where David and family lived and thirty-five minutes from daughter Jenn and her husband." (After feeling uncomfortable with several concerns in the first place she visited), "the next place was so different. They had a one-bedroom apartment with full kitchen and extended living space with a washer and dryer. Within what I paid, I could select one meal a day, but had three choices, so it would fit my dietary needs. It was in a lovely suburban neighborhood. A plus was that when I was visiting and touring, several residents were so welcoming and encouraging."

This for-profit apartment building met many of Cindy's present needs. The company that owns it also has an assisted living facility, about thirty miles away, to which she could go if the need arises. And so, for the foreseeable future, she has found her new home.

Mary Ann and I had lived just a few blocks from Cindy and Gordon for over thirty years. We lived in the same neighborhood and went to the same church. Our decision-making processes have both led us closer to our family members and hundreds of miles from our old neighborhood—in opposite directions.

## The Skilled Nursing Facility/Nursing Home Possibility

When a person develops needs beyond what a multilevel retirement community can provide, or if a person living in one's own home is not able to do so any longer, the option may be a nursing home, also called a skilled nursing facility.

From his perspective as a geriatrician, here is Dr. Dedon's description of the place of nursing homes in aging persons' experience.

*Persons with the most disabilities and need for assistance with their Activities of Daily Living (ADL's) may need to live in a nursing home. For older adults, there may be three levels of ADL:*

*The BADL (basic activities of daily living) describes the ability to feed oneself, ambulate with or without an assistance device, be continent and toilet oneself, and bathe oneself.*

*The IADL (instrumental activities of daily living) describes the ability to remain more independent in society by being able to shop, do housework, prepare food, pay bills, manage finances, communicate with others, use phone or computer, transport oneself by driving, using a bike or using public transportation.*

*The AADL (advance activities of daily living) describes activities that lead to the quality of life, such as paid or volunteer work, family activities, religious activities, hobbies. travel, gardening, exercise, sports activities.*

*Those persons who have deficits in several BADL's or Dementia syndromes with associated behavioral disturbance such as wandering, or those with severe chronic mental illness may require the 24/7 care support. This will probably be in a nursing home. Likely, there will be two patients in a quite small room. (Some states require separate facilities for those with mental illness.)*

*There are about 15,000 nursing homes in the United States. In the nursing home, the care is provided by a CNA, a Certified Nurses Aid. The medications will be given by a medication technician or a LPN, a Licensed Practical Nurse, and the patients' care is generally supervised by the LPN. The RN Registered Nurse is often a supervisor and assistant director of nursing. The general manager of the nursing home is the administrator a position requiring the person to be trained and pass a nursing home administration exam.*

Families and patients may expect the person in the nursing home will be monitored closely and frequently, but often this is not that way. A typical good Nursing Home in the United States provides on the average 4.5 hours per day of total nursing time which includes the managers and administrators. This means that for almost twenty hours per day the patient is in one's chair, bed, wheelchair and on their own. Nursing time with the patient includes transfer from bed to wheelchair to toilet and back, dressings, toileting, bathing, dining with or without assistance, and transfers to activities or apartments. Unfortunately, many nursing homes cannot retain enough CNA's because their pay is low, work is hard, and often they must deal with patients who are incontinent, who are demented, or with agitated and aggressive patients. They also deal with family members who have unrealistic expectations of patient care. A big problem in the Nursing Home industry is the high turnover of CNA's, and chronic shortage of these workers is widespread.

The patient and family often have misconceptions about NH safety. About 30 percent of community dwelling elderly fall each year, and sometimes patients enter a NH because of falls. However, entering a nursing home actually increases the risk of falling with 50 percent of patients in nursing homes, even the best ones, suffering a fall each year.

Nursing homes are evaluated and compared to other in their state and in the United States based on patient characteristics submitted to the government on the Minimum Data Sheet, MDS. The information submitted include patient characteristics such as pressure ulcers, falls, unintended weight loss, incontinence, psychotropic drug use such as antipsychotic drugs. The Nursing Home will receive feedback reports comparing it with others in the state and the United States.

Nursing homes are surveyed yearly by the state oversight agency and periodically by the federal government's Medicare surveyors. They are rated from one star, the lowest, to five stars the highest. Those ratings are available to review at the Medicare website.

Nursing Homes provide long term care but also provide post-hospital rehabilitation. A Medicare A–insured patient who stays in the hospital a minimum of three days and needs post-hospital rehab can go to an acute rehab hospital or unit and have three hours of physical therapy, occupational therapy, speech therapy a day for five days a week. Often a hospitalized Med A patient is already in a Nursing Home or cannot/will not do 3 hours of therapy a day, they will not be admitted.to an acute med rehab unit after hospitalization. If this group needs rehab, they may go to a Skilled Nursing Facility (SNF)-Nursing Home or a Med A unit. They will have one hour of therapy per day five days per week, paid for by insurance such as Medicare A. They must have a post three-day minimum hospital stay. Medicare A will pay for up to 100 days of SNF paying 100 percent of the total cost day 1 to 20, then a copay begins for days 21 to 100. After 100 *days, Medicare A stops paying. The patient must then be healthy and stay out of the hospital for 60 days before Medicare A will grant another 100 days of SNF benefit.*

## Cost Considerations

All along the housing-care continuum for elders, cost is a big piece in making these decisions. Older adults may have been living well within their means and expecting to have some money to meet emergencies if needed, but hopefully to provide to their heirs. Deciding to come to one of these facilities, even a comparatively modestly priced with fewer of the services and amenities will almost certainly have a measure of "sticker shock."

My wife and I certainly experienced that. As part of the admission, we submitted financial statements that indicated we would probably be able to pay for our living quarters and services to the end of our days. Then we paid a "life lease" amount, something in excess of what we received from selling our home. (Our estate will receive 90 percent of the "life lease" when we vacate the apartment. That is, unless that fund has had to be tapped to pay for our care.) Then there is a monthly fee that provides a certain amount for meals, housekeeping services, indoor garage, utilities, life enrichment activities, and other housing needs. There will be other quite large costs if we need rehabilitation services, assisted living, or memory care in the future. Moving beyond hoping to have funds to leave our children and grandchildren, we hope at least to be able to pay for whatever care we might need.

The costs are much greater if an aging person can no longer care for oneself and need the presence of a registered nurse at the facility 24/7. As Dr. Dedon notes of this circumstance:

*Nursing homes are expensive. A typical nursing home costs $70,000 to $80,000 per year. The most common payer source for a U.S. nursing home patient is Medicaid, the federal and state-funded state-administered health insurance for the poor. About 40 percent of nursing home patients have Medicaid paying for their nursing home costs. Private pay with the patient spending their own money for nursing home cost is also common. Private pay patients in nursing homes are in a spend-down mode, spending down their financial assets until they are poor enough to qualify for Medicaid. Qualified military veterans may live in a V.A. nursing home or have the V.A. help pay for nursing home care. Some people have long-term care insurance which will usually pay some nursing home cost for a specific period of time. Last year Medicare A paid for about 14 percent of U.S. nursing home revenues, paying for a patient to be in a SNF for up to 100 days after that qualifying three-day hospital stay.*

## Making Choices—Finding the Right Facility

Whatever level of care is needed, there is still the task of selecting the best possible place to live and receive these services. There are many options, so making the right choice is an important and delicate journey. This is also an ominous task. This is choosing the place, people, and services for where a person will likely spend the rest of one's life!

How can a wise choice be made? For one, referrals and research. One's doctors and nurses, friends who have helped their parents get placed, residents of retirement communities themselves can be asked. They may also provide leads and guides of places and situations to avoid. When researching nursing homes, the website Medicare.gov provides information on safety and quality records.

Another question is availability and cost. When asking about availability, one might also ask how this is handled. For example, we were told that there was, on average, a three-year waiting period after applying. However, those ahead of you can turn down an available apartment and still stay at their spot on the list. So, the apartment we chose came up just a few months later.

If moving to be near family caregivers, the issue of proximity and accessibility to those persons is important. All other things being equal, is one facility closer and easier to access for family and other support groups who care for me?

Tours are another part of information gathering. How well cared for are the facilities? How competent and impressive are staff members? How are residents faring—are they content, enjoying themselves, involved, friendly? What activities are going on and how is the response? What amenities are important, and at what cost? (I quickly learned that retirement communities with swimming pools and water activities cost a good bit more. We chose one without a pool.)

After all that there comes a choice, a decision, legal and financial matters, selling the old home, moving. But that is not the end of it. There is still adjusting and change to do. Liz O'Donnell, author of *Working Daughter* wisely cautions:

"Moving a parent, even a willing one, into a senior living facility is fraught with emotion. Your parents may mourn the loss of their younger years, their independence, and the home they built. They could be scared about aging, making new friends, and finding their way in a new place."[4]

She goes on, speaking to her fellow working daughters, that there are emotions for them as well. They may be questioning their decisions—act too quickly? Wait too long? Overreact? She concludes, "You *will* feel guilt. Know that your feelings are normal and don't need to last forever."[5]

I have seen these challenges in others and in myself. Recently on separate days, both Mary Ann and I encountered a woman named "Char," a new arrival who was lost and confused. There is a long hallway connecting two large buildings of apartments, and she was in the wrong building. Each time, one of us walked her back, visited a bit, and helped her find her door and admit herself to her apartment. We have not heard whether she made the adjustment to being here in independent living or had to have more help. Moving from familiar to unfamiliar can impact a frail older adult more than anticipated.

As for me, I had a day,—a week or so after we moved in,—when a realization hit me that I would not see my friends of the last thirty years again. I did not want to be ungrateful for all the hours of help family had given to get us nicely settled. But I was still teary, depressed, and withdrawn almost into immobility. The worst of it passed in a few days, and I set about trying to find my place in a new community. More than two years later, this sadness comes back from time to time—usually lighter and briefer than the first time.

## FOR REFLECTING AND CONVERSING

1. What conversations have you had about older adult employment—how long to work and at what? What are your thoughts about retirement and employment for yourself?
2. What have you noticed as regards older adults working for wages well into their elder years? Are you aware of why they are doing this—enjoyment or necessity?
3. Are you aware of any ways older adults have found to make a little extra money and have fun doing it? If so, what are they? If not, what might they be? (Several of my older friends worked for a rental car company. They were a pool of drivers who would take cars to where they needed to be. Some of the time between assignments, they sat around drinking coffee and telling stories, on payroll at minimum wage.)
4. How well informed are you about housing and care options for older adults in your community? Who in your community might be knowledgeable and helpful for persons making these decisions?
5. What do you see of older adults still living in their home for many years, even though it has hazardous conditions and heavy maintenance needs? Why do they choose to stay there? What support do they need?

## NOTES

1. Information and statistics came from two sources: Maurice Backman, "The Frightening Reason Many Americans Retire Earlier Than They Planned," accessed December 31, 2019, https://www.msn.com/en-us/money/retirement/the-frightening

-reason-many-americans-retire-earlier-than-planned/ar-BBYungY?ocid=spartanntp; and "Poll: 1 in 4 Have No Plans to Retire," Associated Press, found in *Wisconsin State Journal*, July 8, 2019, A 11.

2. Letter from Jon Dedon, February 2, 2019.

3. Liz O'Donnell, *Working Daughter: A Guide to Caring for Your Aging Parents While Making a Living* (Lanham: Rowman & Littlefield, 2019), 71.

4. O'Donnell, *Working Daughter*, 74.

5. O'Donnell, *Working Daughter*, 75.

*Chapter 6*

# Hear and Respond

## *Our Health and Illness Issues*

So we do not lose heart. Even though our outer nature is wasting away,
Our inner nature is being renewed day by day.

—2 Corinthians 4:16

The vastly increased life expectancy for older adults living in the twenty-first century is good news. The not so good news is that, during these extra years, we older adults have a number of chronic illnesses. At least 80 percent of older adults have at least one chronic health condition; 60 percent have at least two; and a good part of those more than two. (If I include my eye and ear issues, I have at least five, and I am pretty healthy and energetic!) For the most part, we manage that truth well. We don't let it keep us from living with zest and engaging activities that interest us. But there are times we need your help.

I will provide a brief listing and discussion of the most frequent of these health concerns. Caring leaders need at least a basic working knowledge of these problems and their impact. Then I will explore what would be helpful support from a caring community. As in the previous chapter, I am indebted to my friend Dr. Jon Dedon, a highly respected Geriatrician and teacher of Geriatrics at the University of Missouri—Kansas City Medical School. He will elaborate on some of the chronic illnesses I mention. Dr. Dedon's comments will be italicized and indented throughout this chapter.

## OLDER ADULT HEALTH CONCERNS

### Arthritis

Arthritis is one of the most frequent of these chronic illnesses, affecting approximately half of all adults aged over sixty-five. For a good number of us, this can be rather mild, perhaps stiffness, a little pain, and difficulty rising from a sitting or lying condition. It may get better as the day wears on. For others, there is much contortion of the body along with severe pain and body restriction.

*The most common type of arthritis is osteoarthritis. This occurs when the wearing down of protective cartilage on bone ends in joints results in bone on bone impact and inflammation, with pain, stiffness, bony deformity, and loss of joint function. Inflammatory arthritis, such as rheumatoid arthritis or psoriatic arthritis result when the body attacks itself, resulting in joint destruction. These types of arthritis require disease-modifying treatments such as TNF agents or IL agents to reduce the body's attack on itself. Arthritis also results from previous traumatic injuries, such as sports injuries. Exercise, medication, joint injection with steroids, joint surgery and joint replacement surgery all have a role in helping.*

### Osteoporosis

Osteoporosis is a much different bone disease. This is low bone mass, and it can cause persons to be less mobile, and in danger of becoming disabled in the event of a fall, as bones may fracture or vertebrates collapse. It is estimated that fifty-four million Americans over age fifty are affected by low bone mass.

*Osteoporosis is defined as a DEXA scan bone mass more negative than or equal to negative 2.5. Treatment of osteoporosis includes exercise, calcium, Vitamin D, and specific osteoporosis treatments such as bisphosphonates such as Fosamax or other agents such as Prolia.*

### Heart Disease

The next two are more deadly. One of these is heart disease. As a chronic condition, 37 percent of older men and 36 percent of older women have it in some form. There are nearly 500,000 deaths a year associated with heart disease. It is important to know that there have been marvelous strides in medical treatment, which has improved and extended the lives of many.

*Heart disease can occur as coronary artery disease, CAD, or left ventricular failure, called congestive heart failure, CHF or heart rhythm disturbance, or heart valve disease, among other types of heart disease. CAD disease occurs when coronary arteries, the arteries that supply blood to the heart muscle itself become narrowed with plaque. Plaque can develop due to smoking, high cholesterol, high blood pressure, Diabetes Mellitus, and aging. If the person is genetically determined to have small coronary arteries, so much the worse. Angina pectoris, heart pain can be due to narrowed coronary arteries, unable to adequately deliver blood containing oxygen to the heart muscle, and a heart attack—myocardial infarction results when an arterial blockage results in heart muscle death.*

*Left ventricular failure, CHF is caused by a left ventricle that does not pump out enough of its contained blood. This weakened heart pump has a low ejection fraction; it is too weak to pump out an adequate volume of blood. This is called heart failure with reduced ejection Fraction, HFrEF. Sometimes the ejection Fraction as measured by echo cardiogram seems maintained, but the patient still exhibits heart failure. This is called heart failure with preserved ejection Fraction HFpEF. This results from a stiff walled left ventricle unable to distend during its filling period called diastole, resulting in less blood to pump out.*

*Heart rhythm disease often is an irregular heartbeat called atrial fibrillation. A.fib is especially dangerous for increased risk of stroke when small blood clots form in the heart and go into the arterial circulation causing brain artery blockage and stroke.*

*Heart valve disease includes narrowing and calcification of the aortic valve leading out of the left ventricle. If the aortic valve becomes too stenotic, heart failure will result.*

I am one who benefited from the growing knowledge and procedures for heart issues. At the age of sixty-three, I was diagnosed with a blockage in the left descending anterior artery from my heart. My cardiologist performed angioplasty on that blockage and inserted stents. I was told that before this procedure was available, that blockage was known as "the widow maker." (My father died of heart disease at fifty-five.) At one of my annual exams, I was able to thank my cardiologist for twenty good years before I moved from that community, and the count goes on.

For all of us, the advice "exercise, eat well, get a good night's rest" is important. Then, there should be moderation of alcohol consumption and elimination of tobacco. These practices have promise of extending our lives, enriched and lengthened by good medical care.

## Cancer

Cancer, in all its various forms, is the second leading cause of death among older adults. Something in excess of 400,000 die of this disease each year.

It is estimated that in our elder years 28 percent of men and 21 percent of women are affected in some way. The various early screenings and examinations, such as mammograms, colonoscopies, and skin checks, can detect the cancer early and often offer ways to deal with it and slow its course.

> *Traditional cancer treatments have included surgery, chemotherapy, and radiation therapy. We now have more treatment modalities including targeted therapies and immunotherapy. We know most cancers are the result of genetic errors, so evaluating the cancer for its genetic makeup is now the standard. A nonsmoker may develop lung cancer due to a genetic error combining the EML4 gene with the ALK gene. The EML4—ALK gene fusion produces a protein that stimulates and supports lung cancer. Traditional platinum-based combination chemotherapy can help, but often these patients take crizotinib which helps with the gene error protein.*
>
> *Acute leukemia and lymphoma are often treated with chemotherapy and stem cell treatments. When these fail, chimeric antigen, T-cell therapy called CAR-T may help. In CAR-T treatment, the patient's infection fighting T-cells are taken out, given a virus causing them to increase their surface structures such as receptors, making the T-cells much better cancer killers. The T-cells are then reinfused into the patient often helping people otherwise certain to die very soon. Reductions in cancer deaths annually have been going on since the early 1990s.*

## Respiratory Diseases

Respiratory diseases such as chronic obstruction pulmonary disease (COPD) is the next frequent cause of death among people sixty-five and older. Chronic bronchitis and emphysema are other diseases in this category. Together they account for, or are a factor in, about 125,000 deaths a year. Perhaps as many as a tenth of older people contend with these illnesses in some form and degree of severity. These conditions can also make one more vulnerable to pneumonia, which is one of the top eight causes of death for persons over sixty-five.

## Stroke

A stroke happens when the blood stream to some part of the brain is reduced or interrupted.[1] This is a medical emergency and persons are wise to be aware of the symptoms—drooping on one side of the face, inability to raise and hold both arms aloft, slurred or strange speech. Then one should seek emergency help at once.

Types of strokes include the following: hemorrhagic stroke, when a blood vessel in the brain ruptures or leaks; ischemic stroke, when the brain's blood vessels become narrowed or blocked (the most common type); and transient ischemic attack (TIA)—a temporary period of symptoms. This is also known as a ministroke. When one has had a TIA, the risk of a full-blown stroke is greater.

There are many things to do that reduce the threat of stroke: lowering blood pressure and cholesterol; quitting tobacco use; managing one's diabetes; maintaining a healthy weight; and regularly exercising, to name a few. There are also physical and occupational therapy exercises that may help reduce the harmful impact of strokes.

## Parkinson's Disease

According to a Mayo Clinic publication, "Parkinson's disease is a progressive nervous system disorder that affects movement."[2] The symptoms, which vary greatly from person to person, may include tremor or shaking, slowed movement, rigid muscles, speech and writing changes, falls, gait dysfunction, and more.

About one million Americans have Parkinson's, ten million worldwide. Each year, about 60,000 people are diagnosed with PD, and many more go undiagnosed. The mean survival rate after onset is approximately twelve years.

*Parkinson's Disease, P.D., occurs when brain cells, neurons in the substantia nigra region of the brain, become diseased with Lewy Bodies, small inclusion bodies. This reduces production of the neurotransmitter brain chemical dopamine, resulting in Parkinsonism. Exercise and bicycle riding are quite helpful for Parkinson's Disease, including group exercise sessions in boxing clubs. Physical Therapy, Occupational Therapy and Speech Therapy are quite helpful including LSVT Lee Silverman Voice Training – "Big" and "Loud" programs. Medications that help include Sinemet, a traditional carbidopa/levodopa combination, Rytary a new carbidopa levodopa combination, other dopamine agonists such as Requip. A very helpful surgery is the placement of a deep brain stimulator, which can produce dramatic improvement.*

## Diabetes

Diabetes Mellitus is the name for a group of diseases that affect how one's body uses blood sugar (glucose). The most common type among older adults is Type II also known as Adult Onset Diabetes. This is a disease that is readily identified and addressed with blood tests for blood sugar levels.

*A blood test called HgbA1C is used to monitor blood glucose control for a period of months, with a HgbA1C equal to or greater than 6.5 percent diagnostic of Diabetes Mellitus II. Traditionally, HgbA1C goals have been less than 7*

*percent. For frail older adults at risk of too much blood glucose lowering, called*
*hypoglycemia, with risk of fainting, falls, seizures, we now consider HgbA1C*
*equal to or less than 8.0 percent an acceptable goal.*

Diet, weight reduction, and exercise may be sufficient so that the body does not require insulin or other medications. For others, medication may be constant.

Nevertheless, it is a serious ailment. The Center for Disease Control estimates that 25 percent of all people aged sixty-five and over are living with diabetes. It causes in excess of 50,000 deaths among seniors each year.[3]

## Falls

With so many developing health conditions that affect balance and mobility, it need be no surprise that falls—and the damage to one's body from the fall—are a significant health risk among seniors.

Each year 30 percent of people over sixty-five years of age have a fall while living in the community. And quite likely, a significant proportion of this group will be back for a repeated fall within a year. Many of these falls happen in one's home, perhaps due to removable hazards such as area rugs and slippery bathroom floors. I can tell you from firsthand experience and visiting with my friends, there are many more falls than are reported.

Many an older adult who has had a rather enjoyable elderhood finds it suddenly changed when a fall results in a broken hip or other bone. Surgery, including anesthesia (a health hazard itself, riskier for older adults), immobility, and physical therapy will mark a long journey back, and all this may not bring one back to the pre-fall state.

*To reduce fall risk, multiple steps can be taken. Have your health care provider*
*review your medications that have falls risk, such as anxiety or depression*
*medications, sleep medications, cardio-vascular medications, medications that*
*can be intoxicating.*

*Exercise regularly such as walking 25 minutes a day, 5 days a week.*

*Make your home safer. Use good lighting. Have safe well lighted stairs with*
*handrails. Have a bathroom with a nonskid surface for the floor of the shower*
*or tub. Use shower chairs and shower hose. Have a raised toilet seat, use*
*grab bars around the toilet and in the shower. Keep the path between bed and*
*bathroom clear and lighted. Never stand on a chair or step stool in the kitchen.*
*Never go up on a ladder to clean leaves from gutters or put up Christmas lights.*
*Take adequate Vitamin D such as at least 800 IU of Vitamin D3 daily. Discuss*
*falls with your health care provider at least once a year.*

## Eye and Ear Problems

Elders develop many problems with their eyes. With frequent and early attention, these problems can be reduced, and perhaps at least slowed down, so that there may be some eyesight for as long as possible. The four main eye issues that elders face are cataracts, dry eye, glaucoma, and age-related macular degeneration.

Cataracts are cloudy spots of protein molecules on the lens of the eye. Cataract surgery removes the cloudy lens and replaces it. Dry eye happens when the lacrimal glands that produce tears stop working. This possibly may be corrected by a simple procedure.

Glaucoma occurs if there is too much fluid pressure within the eye. When detected it can be treated with a surgical procedure or nightly eye drops. Age-related macular degeneration occurs when the macula, the part of the retina that processes central vision deteriorates. There is also diabetic retinopathy and retinal detachment.

Skilled medical practice can extend the time when one has vision and delay impediments to vision or perhaps restore them, but it requires awareness brought about by regular exams. It has been estimated that 65 percent of adults over fifty years of age have eye problems. Preservation of one's vision is a crucial need for most people's quality of life.

As to hearing issues, it is estimated that one-third of the people between sixty-five and seventy-five years experience some hearing loss, and at least half of those over seventy-five do. There are many causes of hearing loss—loud noises, earwax, or fluid buildup, or a punctured or damaged ear drum. There are a number of types of hearing difficulties including sudden hearing loss, age-related loss (Presbycusis), or ringing in the ears (tinnitus).

*The most common form of hearing loss in older adults is Presbycusis, which is high-frequency sensorineural hearing loss. Often ear wax buildup can be a problem, so treatment with over the counter softeners and lavage can help.*

Sometimes there is limitation in understanding or comprehending even when the words can be heard. Many of these hearing problems can be addressed in at least some measure.[4] At the same time, helps such as hearing aids can cost thousands of dollars and may be beyond the affordable range of some older people.

*Many states have Medicaid programs that will pay for hearing aids. Medicare generally does not, although there are a few programs that do.*

*Chapter 6*

## ONE MORE DIFFICULT HEALTH ISSUE—MEMORY

There is one more health issue that is greatly feared by older people and is also the condition where I experienced some of my worst failures as a pastoral caregiver. I speak of memory loss or dementia. Some people automatically think of Alzheimer's when this subject comes up, but there about sixty different causes of dementia.

> *Acquired cognitive impairment, called dementia, more recently named Major Neurocognitive Disorder, increases in prevalence with increasing age. Alzheimer Disease is the most common type, followed by Vascular Dementia and Lewy Body Dementia, dementia from traumatic brain injury, dementia due to alcoholism (Korsakoff Syndrome), dementia associated with Parkinsonism. In persons younger than 60 years old, Frontotempora dementia is most common. The prevalence of dementia at age 65 is about 1–2 percent but by age 85, that prevalence approaches 50 percent. There are no cures for these dementia diseases currently, but medicine that can cloud the mind, such as medicines like Benadryl as a sleep aid, or oxybutynin as a bladder aid should be discontinued. Regular exercise can help with mood and fitness. Advance planning for health care directives and durable power of attorney for health care are a must. The web site https://alz.org. can be helpful. Trials of medicines like Aricept, Exelon, and Namenda are worth a try. For some they help, for some they do not help, and for some side effects are worse than any benefit.*

The ways that this dementia—or memory loss (many persons' preferred term) are experienced are widely varied. One person could not remember what was said in a conversation one minute earlier. Another could enter into conversation but was completely lost as to space if she stepped outside her apartment alone. One woman assured her family she still knew who they were even if she couldn't remember their names. Another, a man, seemed not to recognize anyone familiar, not even his wife of more than fifty years. One person was confused about many things but played Euchre weekly—and won a lot more than he lost. Another seemed to experience rapid deterioration in all or many aspects—social skills, reading, writing, drawing.

A person with this disease may die as soon as eighteen months or live up to twenty-seven years with it. The average length of surviving with this condition is ten to twelve years.[5]

One of my biggest failures in pastoral care came when an older woman in our congregation began developing symptoms. She, her husband, and her daughter went to an Alzheimer's support group at a nearby hospital—once. They did not return because it was so scary and discouraging.

The woman had been a regular member of the women's group, but when she came, no one sat with her as her dining skills were mostly gone. In a rather short time, she had to be placed in a secure facility. She was among those that we pastors called on. But we were not sure what to do or say. When she died, the family sensed they had been grieving for a long time as the illness attacked more and more of this wife, mother, grandmother they loved.

A short time after her death, at a men's prayer breakfast, her husband exploded at the group, but mostly at me. "You let us down! We have attended and supported this church for years and years, and yet when we needed you most, you let us down!!" I sat there and took it. Basically, I agreed with him. But neither I nor my staff knew what to do or how to do it—beyond our feeble efforts.

One of the dark sides of the increasing longevity of people is that there will be more persons with memory loss—persons and their families who need our compassion, care, and support. And so, what can be offered? Corinne Trevitt, out of her studies, experience, and research replies, "Create a caring environment." This is guidance for the institution, for the family, and for the pastoral caregivers. She suggests this environment includes communication—beyond trivia, down to subjects that might interest the person. Another part of this is personhood, resisting the temptation to conclude the person is "no longer there," but wait and look for ways to connect with the person struggling with this difficulty. It also involves managing pain and encouraging spiritual reminiscence. It is possible that well-informed questions about a person's childhood, including church, religion, times of joy, times of hope may provide a few moments of remembrance and contact.

Out of his wide experience in this ministry, Malcolm Goldsmith considers what are the spiritual needs of a person with dementia, and responds, "Surely to be accepted, to be given worth and honor, to be befriended and to be listened to, to be placed within a wide context of peace and security, of beauty and love . . . with an extra measure of sensitivity."[6]

He goes on to consider the spiritual needs of the family caregivers to a person with dementia, and he responds, "These are people who have cried enough tears to fill a well; they are people who have experienced a lifetime's emotions in the space of a few months or years, and who ask themselves over and over again, 'How can we sing the Lord's song in a strange land?' Here are people hungering and thirsting for a word of hope, for a sense of meaning and who are often wracked by a deep sense of guilt." And, he adds, there is probably exhaustion from the demands of the disease.

As Goldsmith considers pastoral support in these hard experiences, he suggests a new understanding of hope "Hope is not about believing you can change things. Hope is about believing you make a difference."[7]

In chapter 9, we will speak of music therapy as a resource for persons with dementia. In chapter 10, we will tell of "Oasis," a monthly day of safe care for persons with dementia still living in their homes, to give their caregiver three to four hours of respite relief.

There is another caring response that deserves mention. The Due West United Methodist Church of Marietta, Georgia provides support groups for caregivers of persons with dementia. This started as one group. Sharon Welch was asked to lead it out of her experience of caring for her mother through the end of her life with dementia. The power of the loving support propelled them into broader vistas. As the Faith and Leadership website describes it—"What started with a simple support group has grown to include online resources and gatherings that pursue its twofold Mission: to help caregivers and to educate community leaders. It's part of a growing trend of congregations supporting the 'invisible second patients' of dementia."[8] Any who consider the possibility of responding in some way to persons with dementia, perhaps by deeper support of their caregivers need to learn of this ministry. They might be led to attend one of the conferences or be guided by the resources they have developed. The citation above will guide one to this vital ministry and the resources it has developed.

The longer life expectancy is certainly a gift. However, sometimes it is a painful gift. Caring pastor and community are needed to see us through.

## Complicating Factors

There are factors that make many of the maladies I have mentioned worse, harder to treat, and with less success. Two of these are substance abuse (including tobacco) and obesity, hardly problems of the elderly alone. These issues probably started much earlier in life and were hard to overcome. And so, they have continued with disheartening consequences in the elders' search for good enough health.

Younger people who struggle with the same issues will be wise to do two things. For one, address them now so that they will be healthier in old age. For the other, offer a deeper measure of understanding and support to older adults who struggle with ill health and these issues.

A third factor is poverty. In listing the treatments for the various health issues listed in this section, there is always a qualifier—if you can afford it, or if there is an agency that can provide it for you. For too many, the answer is no. For example, in 2013, the Kaiser Family Foundation report said that 45 percent of adults ages sixty-five and older had incomes below the poverty level.[9]

## THEREFORE, WHAT DO WE NEED FROM YOU?

### An Extra Set of Ears and Voice

Recently, I had an appointment with a therapist to diagnose and respond to voice issues I was having. I was fortunate that my daughter Julie, a finely educated nurse, took me and participated in the interview-examination. She helped me tell the therapist things about me and my health history, I had not thought of. She also helped me hear, evaluate, and figure out how to do the voice therapy sessions the therapist recommended. The appointment was so much more effective because of Julie's participation.

For elders who do not have an available family member, perhaps a caring community can offer those ears and voice. It may be a friend, someone who has gone through the same issue, a retired health professional, or one of the church staff.

I probably should also have added "memory" to the list of what such a person provides. This memory flows two ways: to remember health history going into the appointment, and to remember guidance provided by the health care professional.

## Wheels

An older person may also need transportation to appointments and treatments. In one church I served, two younger retirees saw this as part of their ministry and drove many elders to and from their appointments. In some communities, there is such transportation provided. The help needed might be knowledge of this transportation service and guidance as how to enroll for its services and engage it when needed.

## Coordination

Quite often, each of the elder's health conditions is addressed by a specialist. While these specialists' knowledge is invaluable, it can also be confusing. There are appointments with several doctors, and each may offer prescriptions and treatments. This may lead to more confusion—how to remember and attend of all these appointments, how to combine the various treatments suggested, how to keep track of and take all the prescribed medications. And there may be another problem. Perhaps the various prescriptions include some medicines that should not be taken together.

## The Parish Nurse Option

Fortunate is the elder who has knowledgeable family members or friends to help negotiate this complicated journey through health treatment for a variety of issues. Some churches and agencies have discovered an effective way to offer this guidance. They engage the services of a Parish Nurse, one who has been trained in this specific form of nursing.

What does a parish nurse do? A website dedicated to informing about this discipline answers:

Parish nurses provide care within parish/faith communities, incorporating religious beliefs, spirituality and heath care to promote healing and wellness among the members of that community. Parish nurses may provide health care services such as preventative health screening activities or may visit members of their community at home or in the hospital or long-term care facility. They may offer counseling about health care issues, or provide education, promoting preventative care and health maintenance.[10]

> We wither, sag, wrinkle, crinkle, tatter, and become marked by life's events. Time and gravity, air and water wear us down, each into a unique and precious beauty, every bit as beautiful as a landscape or plant, weathered by the seasons.
>
> —Stephanie Sugars

This website also provides contact information for several parish nurse training programs, which provide education in wholistic health, spirituality and health, and more to persons who have their RN credentials.

For a time, Cindy Haynes served as Parish Nurse for a congregation where I was pastor. This was so enriching, particularly to our frail elderly members. Though it was part time and voluntary, it was so helpful. Among the services she offered were these:

- She took blood pressures for any who wanted it on Sundays or at the monthly older adult social gathering.
- She made personal visits with older adults and assessed what would be helpful for them. She also listened to their stories, much enjoyed both by her and by the people she visited.
- She accompanied a few on their doctor's visits, particularly those who didn't have a family or friend to go with them.
- Once, during her time with us, she organized a health fair, recruiting knowledgeable people in several health areas both from within the church and in the community and offering the fair both to church people and to the community.
- She made hospital visits as needed.

There was one time especially when her presence at the hospital was much needed. An elderly woman had fallen in her apartment during the night, and she had lain for quite some time before help arrived. The hospital staff found her extremely combative and resistant. When Cindy arrived, she assured them that was not her normal behavior. At her suggestion, they visited with the patient and learned of a medication that was the problem.

Her combination of a deep faith, a caring presence, and wide nursing training and experience made her contribution to the life and welfare of persons in the community so valuable.

## AND SO

In this chapter, I have offered a brief description of many—though probably not all—of the health issues we older adults may undergo, and where we may need your help and that of others in our faith community. These descriptions have been elaborated at times by a geriatrician. We usually make our peace with these issues most of the time, and we lead interesting lives in spite of them. But there are times we need your presence, care, and support. I trust you will be there for us.

Further, someday each of us will be dying—likely from one of these illnesses. Or perhaps we will be the survivor of a partner or friend who died. We will need you then as well. But I will delay discussion of those matters until chapters 11 and 12. However, before that, we have much learning, growing, serving, and giving to do. We will turn to these topics in the next few chapters.

## FOR REFLECTING AND CONVERSING

1. What meaningful encounters have you had in ministering with people experiencing some of the chronic illnesses mentioned —or others? What, if anything, complicates this aspect of ministry for you?
2. Among the people you know, who is the most gifted person in offering ministry to people with any of these chronic diseases and their families? What makes them so? What can you learn from them?
3. What has been your experience in ministering with people who have dementia? With their caregivers? With their families? Who or what can teach you and guide you in this ministry?
4. What is your response to Malcom Goldsmith's suggestion that "Hope is believing you can make a difference"?
5. What, if any, has been your experience with a Parish Nurse? How do you respond to the concept of Parish Nurses? What benefits would it have for your ministry? Does anyone come to mind who could fill that role—perhaps someone retired, perhaps part-time, perhaps voluntary, or?

## NOTES

1. "Stroke," accessed March 31, 2020, https://www.mayoclinic.org/diseases-conditions/stroke/symptoms-causes/syc-20350113.

2. "Parkinson's Disease," accessed March 31, 2020, https://www.mayoclinic.org /diseases-conditions/parkinsons-disease/symptoms-causes/syc-20376055.

3. "About Diabetes," accessed April 4, 2020, https://www.cdc.gov/diabetes/b asics/diabetes.htm.

4. "Hearing Loss: A Common Problem for Older Adults," accessed March 31, 2020, https://www.nia.nih.gov/health/hearing-loss-common-problem-older-adult.

5. Corinne Trevitt, "Chapter 8, Meeting the Challenge: Older People with Memory Loss and Dementia," in *Spiritual Growth and Care in the Fourth Age of Life*, edited by Elizabeth MacKinlay (London: Jessica Kingsley Publishers, 2006), 111.

6. Malcom Goldsmith, "Through a Glass Darkly: A Dialogue Between Dementia and Faith," in *Aging, Spirituality and Pastoral Care: A Multi-National Perspective*, edited by Elizabeth MacKinlay, James Ellor, and Stephen Pickard (New York: Haworth Press, 2001), 130.

7. Goldsmith, "Through a Glass Darkly," 132, 133.

8. "Dementia Ministry in Georgia Serves as a Model for Churches to Care for the Caregivers," accessed April 5, 2020, https://faithandleadership.com/dementia-minis try-georgia-serves-model-churches-care-caregivers.

9. Madeline R. Vann, "The 15 Most Common Health Concerns for Seniors," accessed April 5, 2020, https://www.nia.nih.gov/health/hearing-loss-common-prob lem-older-adult.

10. "What is a Parish Nurse?" accessed April 11, 2020, https://rncareers.org/career /parish-Nursing/#-how-do-parish-nurses-earn.

# Chapter 7

# Help Us Explore

## *Why Am I (Still) Here?*

Let each of you lead the life that the Lord has assigned, to which God called you.

—1 Corinthians 7:17

The two most important days in your life are the day you were born and the day you find out why.

—Mark Twain[1]

Who will I be when I can no longer do the work that has been a primary source of identity for me for the past half century?

—Parker Palmer[2]

When we minister with older adults, we need to be aware of a deep question that may be spoken or unspoken. This question may be close to the surface or deep underneath. It is this:

"As I age, as I am no longer employed, as my health, strength, and mobility fades, as people I have loved die, I wonder, why am I here? Why am I still here?"

It is often a painful and lonely question. And it recurs in different forms throughout the years of older adulthood.

Of course, each person must find an answer for oneself. At the same time, there are at least two helpful perspectives a pastoral caregiver can offer. Or, at least, a religious leader can speak with searchers out of these perspectives.

One is the Christian concept of vocation, and the other is found in the perspectives of logotherapy and the search for meaning. At least, these provide a beginning. We will consider each of these and then see where we are on these questions of why am I here?

## VOCATION

Through much of one's life, hours and days have been filled with activities—to earn a living, to care for persons we call family, and, perhaps, to do some activities that serve others. The word "vocation" that comes from the Latin meaning "called" or "summoned," gathers together those various activities that have filled those days.

Quite often, the most basic way the word "vocation" was used was for one's employment. For a long time, this part of a person's vocation has occupied the largest part of one's attention, time, and energy.

But then, there comes a time when that main activity of our lives comes to an end. When? As we mentioned in a previous chapter, the traditional time has been at sixty-fiveyears of age, though this varies with the occupation. Recently, social security has been moving the age of retirement upward toward sixty-seven where one receives full benefits.

Those who are vigorous in their "young old" years—for ten or more years after sixty-five—may enjoy demanding activities, and/or engage in much volunteerism, and/or launch an "encore career."

Sooner or later, one's work comes to an end of first career and possible encore careers. What then? Mary Pipher has noted, "The loss of work has killed many a person." Males may experience this most urgently, particularly if they have few interests or friends outside of work. There will be new questions about what to do with one's time? There will be a need to find one's place in family and society. However, she notes, "Women, who are used to second-shift work generally fare better. Many of their jobs stay with them till they die."[3]

Depending on whether one enjoyed the work or was feeling stressed and overwhelmed, retirement may feel quite different. Joan Chittister observes "In an age where two out of every five workers are forced to stop working earlier than they planned, the disorientation has all the marks of a social epidemic."[4]

George Vaillant explored the impact of retirement on the people he observed in his longitudinal studies. He concludes that while retirement is a difficult time for some, it can be a rewarding time if four things are true. For one, they need to replace their work associates with another social network. Second, they need to rediscover how to play. Third, they are wise if they cultivate creativity in whatever way appeals to them. And fourth, they should continue lifelong learning.[5] That is a lot of changing and growing to do! It is not surprising that some stumble their way through this transition.

> You are never too old to set another goal or to dream a new dream.
>
> —C. S. Lewis

With many two-career marriages, rarely are both able to retire at the same time, and so adjustments need to be made unique to their situation. For example, who has the heavier schedule, and who is now responsible for household, yard, and socializing tasks?

If the wife had retired earlier or was not employed outside the home, there is a different challenge—as the adage put it, "I took him for better or worse, but not for lunch." Or as one woman noted, retirement meant "twice as much husband and half as much money."[6] For many, finances are a crucial situation. Whether there is scarcity or plenty, there is a new pattern of income and money management, including saving against an uncertain future, to be learned.

Single persons will have their own issues dealing with retirement. Alone, they will need to find relational community, make financial adjustments, and discover the interests, efforts, and causes that appeal.

Once retired into the season of elderhood, what is next? It may be time to move into the larger meaning of "vocation." The Random House dictionary has further definitions of vocation—"a calling or summons, as to a particular activity or career," and "a divine call to God's service or to the Christian life," and "a function or station to which one is called by God."[7]

Parker Palmer has noted, "The way I've earned my keep has changed frequently but my vocation has remained the same." (He defines his vocation as learner-teacher-and, most of all, writer.) He goes on to counsel "As we grow older, it's important to get clear about the difference between a job and a vocation. Too many older folks . . . fall into despair because they lose not only their primary source of income . . . but their sense of identity as well."[8] A person can have a job to make a living, or a job as part of a vocation that will endure, even after the employment ends.

It is important to look at one's present situation and ask what one's vocation is in this new time of life. Perhaps there is a new living situation, a new community. The question may be phrased thus: In this time and place and in the light of my health and other circumstances, what and where is my calling, my vocation? How do I find my way into that verse from Corinthians, "Let each of you lead the life that the Lord has assigned, to which God called you"? Why am I here? Why am I still here? (And it may be helpful for a pastor to raise these questions and help the elder see the possibilities.)

Ruth Rosell noted that in her conversations, older adults rarely talked about their work life. Rather, many talked about their family and those relationships that had become more needed and more meaningful. They spoke of their enthusiasm for using their skills and interests in the present. A few examples: persons have enjoyed being volunteers in a hospital, a library, or a grade school. Two early retirees did much calling on the older adults who had been leaders when they first came to the church, and they provided for those elders' transportation needs. One of them also found great delight and spent hours being with his grandsons, teaching them new skills.

Perhaps even more pressing than awakening older adults to their present vocation is the need for society and its institutions to see and make room for the vocations of its elders.

Linda Fried, the geriatrician head of Columbia's School of Public Health has written, "Too many of my patients suffered from pain, far deeper than the physical, caused by not having a reason to get up in the morning. Many of my patients wanted to make a difference in the world but, finding no role for themselves, were treated as socially useless and even invisible."[9]

Pioneer and Pulitzer Prize–winning gerontologist Robert Butler noted, "The tragedy of old age is not the fact that each of us must grow old and die, but that the process of doing so has been made unnecessarily and at times excruciatingly painful, humiliating, debilitating, and isolating."[10]

Karen Scheib sees this blindness in churches at times. She speaks of Sarah who had been an effective schoolteacher with an expertise in working with behavior-disordered children. She had also been a prominent lay leader in her church.

After retiring at sixty-two, Sarah felt as if she aged ten years in six months in the eyes of those who recruited leadership for the church. She felt as if she was no longer considered for important roles in the church. As Scheib summarized, "The church reinforced the cultural narratives of retirement as a time of disengagement and diminishing competence." Rather, Sarah wisely saw "retirement as a time of transition and discernment rather than disengagement."[11] Scheib perceptively describes this experience as "narrative mismatch."

Religious caregivers may richly serve persons helping them ask and work on response to such questions as—why am I here? Why am I still here? What is my vocation; what are my vocations, here and now? The church leader may also be wise to invite persons to consider new aspects of their vocation in service of their church and community. And, help the church and other communities to be aware of the rich gifts that may be experienced as older adults find and act on their vocations.

## LOGOTHERAPY AND THE SEARCH FOR MEANING

Another resource for religious leaders to help older adults work through this issue of meaning late in life is offered by Viktor Frankl and his concept of logotherapy. Frankl was a Holocaust survivor, and, after the war, he applied the insights gained from living through that terrible ordeal into a new psychological perspective. He called it logotherapy, which basically means therapy through helping a person activate one's will to meaning.

As he reflected on what he discovered in those horribly hard days in a concentration camp, he said that a person needed two things to survive: a hope for the future; and some purpose or cause to pursue. He would often quote Nietzsche, "He who has a *why* to live for can bear almost any *how*."[12]

In the therapy he created out of his experiences, he pointed to three kinds of values in which an individual may find meaning. First, there are creative values—creating a work or doing a deed. These are the results of acts or accomplishments that may add to the world's knowledge or to the welfare of humankind. However, creative values are not limited to the highly accomplished person. A person doing basic things such as preparing a simple meal, cleaning the kitchen and bathrooms, or making a bed, may have made life more livable for another—a creative value.

Second, there are experiential values—experiencing something or encountering someone. Simply to know love and friendship with another, or delight in a baby or child, opens one to these experiential values. Being sensitive to truth or beauty—whether in nature, visual arts, or lovely music—is another way. Becoming aware of the goodness and kindliness of a saintly person enriching other lives is still another.

Third, there are attitudinal values—the perspective we take in face of life's reverses. When one is confronted by the fact of uncontrollable suffering or death, there is opportunity to find meaning in the attitude with which one endures those difficult experiences. While all three of these values are important, Frankl said that "attitudinal values are the highest possible values." He went on to explain, "Life never ceases to hold a meaning, for even a person who is deprived of both creative and experiential values is still challenged by a meaning to fulfill, that is by the meaning inherent in an upright way of suffering."[13]

Frankl further cautioned that, if possible, one should not try to find all of the meaning in one's life in a single one of the three values he has identified. Instead, it is wise to seek meaning in as many ways and in as many of these values as possible. Of course, life events may reduce one's way to experience some of these values, but there are still attitudinal values a person may grasp.

He once summarized all this in a slightly different way:

"Life can be made meaningful in a threefold way: first through *what we give* (in terms of creative works); second by *what we take* (from the world in terms of our experiencing values); and third, through the *stand we take* toward a fate we can no longer change (an incurable disease, an inoperable cancer, or the like)."[14]

Frankl was born in 1905. After surviving the Holocaust, he lived to a good old age, dying in 1997 in the ninety-third year of his life. And so, he had ample opportunity to reflect on what his therapy offered in other times and conditions.

Near the end of his life, he wrote an autobiography and reflection, which include thoughts on his aging. In part, he wrote, "I don't mind getting old. As I say, aging does not bother me as long as I have reason to believe that I am still maturing." And again, "In the last analysis, getting old is an aspect of the transitoriness of human existence. But this transitoriness can be a strong motivation for our responsibleness—our recognition of responsibility basic to the human condition."[15]

He was able to claim this perspective and offer guidance and solace to other older adults. For example, one time he was counseling with an elderly physician who was so depressed and lonely after the death of his wife. After listening for a while, Frankl asked the old man, "What would have happened if you had died first, rather than your wife?" The old physician answered, "How she would have suffered." Frankl then said to him, "Don't you see, that great suffering has been spared her, and it is you who have spared her this suffering; but now, you have to pay for it by surviving and mourning her."[16] With his grieving pain reframed in this larger perspective, he saw the purpose in it and resolved to go on. The old man shook his hand and left.

Why am I here? Why am I still here? Look at the interesting and helpful things I do. Think about my relationships, the people I love. Reflect on what of art, humor, entertainment, music still delights me. Look at what I give when I address my pain, suffering, incurable illnesses with peace and courage. Or as Frankl said—our creative, experiential, and attitudinal values. More on this shortly.


## STILL DEEPER


The question "Why am I still here?" becomes even more severe and harsh for those persons who survive to old, old age. They may outlive the activities and usefulness they once enjoyed, and they have lost practically all their friends and family to death.

Archie Ivy thinks of persons in his predominantly African American congregation who are in this circumstance. He reflects, "Lots of seniors are lonely people." Thinking of one person in particular, he comments, "Not only her family, all the people she talked to in the church are gone. Gone also are the teaching and leadership roles she once had in the church." How did he respond to this lonely and bereaved person? "Listen, be sensitive to her needs and desires. Have patience to work with her. She didn't want my pity. She wanted to be heard and to be supported."[17]

Michelle Peterson, director of spiritual services in a retirement community responds similarly. She recalls, "When an older adult struggles with 'why am I still here? Why does God have me here?' I remind them of their purpose, that there is something God still has for them. I share examples from the Bible of people God chose when they were in their upper years. I encourage them to see how beautiful they are. I do not discount how they are feeling. This is very real to them. I try to remind them of God's promises."[18]

Wayne Shannon, chaplain in a retirement community reflects, "Part of my job as chaplain is to help people in change of life situations to move through that. We walk through the darkest valley, but we do not stay there. All have these wilderness periods, especially as we age. I have to remind them that when in one's nineties, they are not in their sixties anymore. Aging becomes more of a reality. The end of life is coming. Though they have lost friends and spouse, going on is going to be ok. A lot of them ask 'why am I still here?' I answer, 'You are here to be a blessing to others. What can I do, what can you do to be a blessing in this life?'"[19]

What do you take from these reflections by three sensitive religious caregivers of older adults? I hear them saying that when there are no easy answers for frail and struggling older adults, there is presence, there is listening, there is respect for the questioner and the question, and, in all this, there is hope.

We will carry this conversation a step further in the next chapter when we explore passions and legacies of older adults.

## QUESTIONS FOR REFLECTING AND CONVERSING

1. What do you see as to how persons you know experience retirement? Do they engage the four steps that Vaillant suggested early in this chapter? How does your congregation/agency respond to them? Do you undervalue them, over work them, or find unique ways to claim their gifts in their new setting? What have you discovered, and what can you teach the rest of us?

2. How might you engage the Christian concept of vocation as described in this chapter to help older adults in their questions and struggles?

3. How might you utilize Frankl's concept of logotherapy and the various values to converse with older adults about their present life and dilemmas?

4. How did you evaluate the responses of religious caregivers to the oldest of the old in the wintry final chapters of their life? What do you do and say when confronted with such questions?

5. How do you answer the question, "Why am I here?" for yourself? What do you imagine will be the hardest times to find an answer to that question? How will you answer it then?

## NOTES

1. As quoted in Bergstrom and Bergstrom, *Third Calling*, 15.

2. Palmer, *On the Brink of Everything*, 267.

3. Pipher, *Another Country*, 175.

4. Joan Chittister, *The Gift of Years: Growing Older Gracefully* (New York: Bluebridge, 2008), 9.

5. George E. Vaillant, *Aging Well* (New York: Little, Brown, and Company, 2002), 224, 238–39.

6. Stevens, *Aging Matters*, 16.

7. *Random House Unabridged Dictionary* (New York: Random House Reference, 1994),1363.

8. Palmer, *On the Brink of Everything*, 85–86.

9. Quoted in Aronson, *Elderhood*, 310–11.

10. Quoted in Aaronson, *Elderhood*, 399.

11. Scheib, *Challenging Invisibility*, 68–69.

12. Viktor E. Frankl, *Man's Search for Meaning: An Introduction to Logotherapy* (New York: Washington Square Press, 1963).

13. Viktor E. Frankl, *The Will to Meaning*, 70 as quoted in Melvin A. Kimble (ed.), *Viktor Frankl's Contribution to Spirituality and Aging* (New York: The Haworth Pastoral Press, 2000), 39.

14. Viktor E. Frankl, *The Doctor and the Soul: From Psychotherapy to Logotherapy* (New York: Vintage Books, 1986), xi. Italics his.

15. *Viktor Frankl Recollections*, 122–23, 124, as quoted in Kimble (ed.), *Viktor Frankl's Contribution*, 4.

16. Kimble (ed.), *Viktor Frankl's Contributions*, 109.

17. Archie Ivy, personal interview October 4, 2019.

18. Interview with Michelle Peterson, September 30, 2019.

19. Wayne Shannon interview, November 26, 2019.

*Chapter 8*

# Help Us Recognize and Claim
# Our Passions and Legacies

So even to old age and gray hairs, O God, do not forsake me, until I proclaim your might to all the generations to come.

—Psalm 71:18

The best use of life is to spend it for something that outlasts life.

—William James[1]

When we come to the subjects of passions and legacies, the mutual ministry between older adults and their religious leaders comes most clear. As religious leaders, we aspire to good quality of leadership and depth of care in the present. We also hope to help build good and enduring foundations for the future of these ministries.

At the same time, we older adults have many things we have cared about all our lives. These include interests, persons, programs, ministries, causes, perhaps a faith including a faith community with its mission, and more. We would like to keep these concerns going and are passionate about their present and future. Perhaps, we would like to share some of the skills, artistry, interests that we have enjoyed with those who may keep that interest or skill alive.

Roland Martinsen notes that passions are "compelling interests." He interviewed a number of elders where he asked about their passions. He noted how the pursuit of their passions energizes and influences not only their lives but also the lives of others.[2]

The older adults he interviewed spoke of a wide variety of passions. These included:

- friends and friendships,
- community projects, such as a preschool or library,
- reading and books,
- writing—memoirs, poetry, humor, and more,
- music—singing, teaching, enjoying; arts, theatre, and concerts, including sharing them with some who would not otherwise be able to experience them,
- leadership—cheerleading a program that will benefit children in his community,
- volunteering for a variety of community and outreach causes,
- a circle of prayer singing—for the support and healing of self and others,
- restoring old tractors,
- enjoying a game such as golf with friends,
- farming and soil conservation—passing well-care for land to the next generation,
- travel, learning, and teaching.[3]

Martinson tells of a couple, Dan and Betty who early in retirement went on a church mission trip to Haiti and were deeply moved by the experience. This has led to many mission involvements. Dan refurbishes computers and distributes them in many countries of need. Further, he has supervised electrical wiring of schools and hospitals in at least five different countries. Betty engages women in sewing and quilting, bringing different groups together around this interest and sometimes giving women a new livelihood.[4]

Their example leads to some important questions and possible strategies for religious leaders. If one is serving a community that has a growing majority of elders, how can this situation be engaged for good? May it possibly be recognizing the passions of these older persons, encouraging them, engaging them, and enlisting them? This can be both for the present effectiveness and the future promise of the church and its many ministries.

The passions I mentioned may at the same time be persons' legacies—or part of their legacies. These two terms, passions and legacies, are so similar, related, and overlapping. The way I am using them here is this: passions refer to present interests and activities that one loves enjoys and feels strongly about. These passions may be about hobbies and activities, about places, about families, or about faith community and its various missions. These passions may have impact on one's influences in

> If there's one thing I've learned in my years on this planet, it's that the happiest and most fulfilled . . . people have devoted themselves to something greater and more profound than themselves and not merely to their own self-interest.
>
> —John Glenn

the future after one dies. On the other land, legacies are more direct attention to the ways one wants to influence and contribute after one's death. Concern for legacies probably begins with passions—activities and interests in the present.

Gerontologist Robert N. Butler defines legacy as "a desire, so profound in older people, to leave something behind them when they die." He notes further "Human beings tend to feel a sense of completion and accomplishment if they can arrange to leave a legacy behind after their death."[5]

And so, another area of worthy inquiry for religious leaders may be to ask, "What do you want your legacy to be?" An even better question may be "What do you want your *legacies* to be?" For as one lives into the future, there possibly are many legacies of several different kinds.

When I interviewed ministers with older adults and asked what they saw among the people in their care, a number spoke of elders' passion and hope that their church would continue to live and offer the gifts of comfort, fellowship, and service they had received to others.

In his congregation, Patrick Roberts sensed despair among elderly members that they could no longer do what they once did to help their church thrive. "I tell them about Abraham, and about King David," he said. "Both were 'seasoned' men. But God used them and many older persons. Just read their Bibles. They will see God can use us all."

He also reminds these elderly members that their support of their minister who represents the church helps continue their passion. They provided the funds needed for his training in prison ministry. "I represent them in the prisons I visit. Their legacy goes on."

Retirement community chaplain Michelle Peterson notes that her elderly residents "want to leave a legacy of hope for younger generations. We live in an age where we are experiencing so much negativism and schism. They hope for their families. Their faith is still there."

Ruth Rosell observes grandparents making an effort to bring and involve their grandchildren in the teachings and ministries of the church. She comments, "I see a number of people—their children may not be involved in church, perhaps due to work, but the grandparents are bringing their children to church and religious activities. What is most important to them is that their faith would be passed on to the next generation and the generation after that."

She also sees the current cohorts of older adults offering a legacy in this time of environmental crisis and global warming. She notes, "Older adults have a perspective on how to live with lots less consumer things, a legacy of living simply."

With these many hopes and commitments, what kinds of legacy are there? The first type of legacy that may come to mind is the financial one. This may be monies to persons or institutions or a cause without specific instruction on how to use it, or it may be money to provide a specific object or activity. People might be remembered with a park bench, a library collection, funding for a food bank, a stain glass window—the possibilities are endless. When I retired from seminary teaching, I was honored with a scholarship in my name. I had a thought on how I would like it used, and family and friends gave additional funds to make this possible. I wanted the scholarship sufficiently funded to do one thing—each year, offer a full scholarship for one course to a potential student to try and see if seminary education is where they are being led. I am delighted that this is happening now and will continue after I am gone.

A Wisconsin newspaper tells of the generous legacy left by Alice Schmidt, a former schoolteacher, later member of the board of education, and always an enthusiast for things educational in the Columbus (WI) School District. Before she died, she requested that her home and all her personal items be gifted to the Columbus School District. And so, the newspaper announced a date for a sale when her well maintained three-bedroom house and her belongings would be auctioned off. These included rare antiques, collectibles, a doll collection, and many history books. All the proceeds were to go into the Alice Schmidt Endowment Fund administered by the school district. Superintendent Annette Deuman commented on what this legacy will mean. "The endowment has been set up, and that fund will begin administering grants in the spring of 2021," she said. "Those grants will be given to any staff member in the district who would like to continue further professional development, and education to become more a master of their craft, whatever that might be. It can be any staff member."[6]

A New England author also found a way to provide a unique legacy. Elizabeth Marshall Thomas wrote and published a best-selling book *The Hidden Life of Dogs*. With income from it she bought the lovely Cunningham Pond in Peterborough, New Hampshire and donated it to the town. She had one stipulation, that there be a beach for humans and a beach for dogs. Thomas Moore who tells of it has often enjoyed that gift, particularly watching the wonderful time the dogs are having on their beach.[7]

Large or small, financial legacies help many a church, agency, or institution survive, thrive, sometimes do something special, and continue its mission.

But legacies can have so many different forms. Thomas Moore recalls that when his father was in his late seventies, he wrote a letter that contained not only practical information for after his death but also reflections on his life and what he was feeling. Moore treasures that letter and will be sure that his children have it in their time.[8] Letters, writings, reflections may be such gifts.

Some time ago, I became deeply aware of what a different world I lived in as a child and youth from that of my grandchildren. In my childhood, we were extremely poor and lived in a small four-room house, with no running water or inside bathroom. We were kept warm by a stove in the living room, fueled by soft, dusty lignite coal. This was in a tiny town on the plains of western South Dakota.

And so I wrote a little book for my six grandchildren and gave it a title inspired by Laura Ingalls Wilder, *Little House in a Little Town on the Prairie*. My sister Ruth and I also wrote about the lives and legacies of our parents, Rev. Ole and Hazel Olson, included the genealogical information we had, and gave copies of that to each member of our extended family. These were our attempts to leave a legacy of understanding, honoring, and appreciating our family heritage.

My sister also participated and sometimes led a memoir writing group in her retirement community. As a part of this, she wrote her memories of many experiences and relationships in her life. All of these are legacies so that family can remember who she was and what she stood for, and in some way, perpetuate those causes dear to her.

Legacy can be an art, a skill, and this includes not only on the objects made and given to others but also the teaching of that gift to others. My wife Mary Ann, a gifted quilt artist, has a rich legacy in both these ways. She has made a beautiful unique Christmas stocking for each member of our extended family as they were born or married into our family. She has also made quilts for so many events—births, graduations, and especially weddings. These are some variation of the wedding ring pattern in colors chosen by the couple. For the last two, she partnered with our daughter Laurie on these.

She also has a legacy of inspiring and encouraging this craft and art in others. For years, she had a "quilt camp" with one daughter and two grand-daughters who all were interested in quilting. Further, she has guided and counseled with many others in their quilting.

In a similar way, people may offer a legacy of their music. My mother was a good country church pianist, and she paid for piano lessons for me. Though I was a poor piano student, I was so excited and entranced when I had a chance to learn to play the baritone horn in the high school band. She and I often played together for church and other events. We practiced a lot more at home—often trying to do works a little beyond us. When we struggled, we were so kind and patient with each other. Eventually, we usually were able to master the more difficult piece. It was a bonding time between mother and me during my difficult high school years. To this day when I see a parent and child playing together, I think of her.

Legacies can be quite subtle. Thomas Moore remembers his mother's Rose of Sharon tree—each place he moves, he plants one in his mother's memory. Scents can be legacies—each time I smell cinnamon rolls baking, I remember two wonderful cooks, my mom and Mary Ann's grandmother.

People can be legacies—a person or a family. People can hope that the family they created and raised and influenced will be an extension of their values and faith. Or the influence on another, say a mentor-mentee relationship, can be a legacy. In this regard, I think of the Rev. Jeannie Sherman. She became my pastor when I was eleven, shortly after my pastor father died. She encouraged my call to ministry, guided me in my choice of college and seminary, and was a wise counselor to whom I turned from time to time in ministry as our friendship continued. She died fifty years after I met her—when I was sixty-one. When she died, in my grief, I called my best friend Ron. He had met her and knew of her importance to me. I told him of her death, and I treasure his response. "Dick, she left a lot of gifts, and you are one of them." He was so right. I am a part of her legacy.

While one aspect of a legacy is what a person is offering others, it is also true that being attentive to legacy is a gift to oneself. As Thomas Moore so helpfully notes, "Feeling that you have a valuable legacy to leave the world, your family, or particular people makes old age more bearable. It can give you a taste of immortality. Your influence will go on, a least for a while, after your passing." And further "A legacy can activate your heart and expand your vision."[9] Not only that, a legacy can be a joy and a sense of fulfillment. These legacies can be large or small. They will be given with the hope of having been significant to someone.

When I think of passions and legacies, my mind goes to a particular older adult whom I loved and enjoyed. She so enriched my life and many others for the years we knew her. Her name was Margaret. She was a retired public health nurse who had served in many parts of the world. Margaret had married late in life and was childless. And so, her family was her church. Her friends were the many people she reached out to, with kindness, hospitality, care, and enthusiasm.

Her passions were numerous. For example, she had a concern for people were diagnosed with diabetes. When she heard of a person with this diagnosis, she would give that person a year's subscription to a diabetes magazine that would provide information and support. She was also an enthusiastic supporter of the United Nations Day Dinner. Year after year, she bought the first table, front and center and invited guests to fill it. This often included Mary Ann and me. Each year, many leaders of community would come by to greet her there. This would include a former mayor, university professors, community leaders, and more.

When she heard of a nursing student or a new nurse, she would want to meet them. Characteristically, she would invite them to a lovely lunch in one of her favorite restaurants to talk, share stories, and offer encouragement.

One of the stories we loved to hear her tell was from the 1940s or 1950s. At that time, there was a "white" nurses' organization and a "black" nurses' organization in Kansas City. She was president of the white contingent, and they had a nationally famous speaker coming to their banquet. Their colleagues in the black association wanted very much to hear the speaker as well. And so, Margaret went to the manager of the segregated hotel and told him they wanted both white and black nurses to come to their upcoming banquet in one of the hotel ballrooms. He allowed that maybe the black nurses could come up the freight elevator out back. She indignantly responded that they would come in the front door, would be met by her nurses' group and escorted up to the ball room. That is what they did, and for one evening at least, she integrated a very segregated hotel!

No one knew how many causes and people she was supporting. When a young man turned to her, among others, to contribute finances in support of his traveling with a religious music group, she responded and hoped this would be a growing experience for him.

She was also a vital and lively member, a past officer, of the local chapter of the American Association of University Women. One time, she persuaded them to invite me to speak to the group, telling one of my Christmas stories. My friend and successor, Heather enjoyed her frequent invitations and warm inclusion at those stimulating events.

Margaret was also enthusiastic about her church and its ministers. Heather recalls her supportiveness, recalling, "She made it clear that a woman in ministry was a good thing, overdue and honorable." I remember that after seasonal or other special events, she would often say to me, "I think this is the best service we ever had."

When she could no longer drive, she would take a taxi to church, knowing she would find people who would share a meal together and take her home. One Sunday, when she called for a taxi, the only vehicle available was a large, long black limousine. This touched her spirit of play, and so she had it take her to church. She was disappointed that there was only one person, Pete who was ushering, that saw her arrival. She walked up and told him "spread it around." She called me that afternoon to tell me about it. She learned the driver's name and engaged that limousine for fun once in a while.

When she died, as she had instructed her attorney, her body was donated to a medical school, and the balance of her pledge to the church was paid for that year.

Some years later, Pastor Heather received a letter from Margaret's attorney. This letter said that Margaret had instructed that her two elderly sisters be provided for until they died. With any remaining funds, half of it was to be given to the nursing school she attended and a half to Prairie Baptist Church. The church would receive some $350,000!

There was no instruction or stipulation on how it was to be used—she let the church figure that out, from the passions and legacies of her life. This led to a lively time of remembering, storytelling, and discernment. Their many conversations explored such questions as how can we be as gracious as she was? And how should we use this and be faithful to what that unforgettable woman had loved and believed in?

It was decided to appoint a Margaret James Estate Mission Fund team to lead a discernment process. The first decision was to divide the gift into three ways: one-third would be devoted to mission objectives; one-third given to the church's capital funds campaign; and one-third to the Prairie Baptist Church Endowment Fund, against future emergencies.

The committee then invited church members to submit requests and suggestions for fitting ways to use that part of the money designated for mission objectives. These should be for mission projects that would embody both Margaret's spirit and the mission commitment of the congregation. When the requests came in, this committee prayerfully considered all requests and made decisions about where to place these funds.

On a lovely summer Sunday in 2010, the church gave away these gifts. Some of the proposals supported were these: scholarships for deserving inner-city high school students and for seminary students; support for mission trips to Philippines, Thailand, and Hong Kong; funds for surgical instruments to treat women in Africa suffering with the fistula medical condition; funding for a Christian Center to initiate a human sex trafficking prevention program; living expense support for a young man awaiting a lung transplant; portable wall partitions for housing families in the interfaith hospitality network, and on and on.

I was present at the joyful Sunday worship service when the grants were given to these various ministries. A representative from each group would accept the gift, thank the church, and tell about the over and above services they would render with the gift. Heather recalls, "My goal was that we might give in a spirit like Margaret's—caring about others, not needing to toot our own horn, investing wisely, experiencing joy." As we sang the last hymn, I felt tears in my eyes, missing Margaret and treasuring her generous impact. As I tried to keep singing, a quote from Margaret came into my mind, "I think this is the best service we ever had."

## FOR REFLECTING AND CONVERSING

1. What memories did the stories in this chapter stir for you? What legacies have benefited you and/or some cause or community important to you?
2. How would you describe the atmosphere and conversation about passions and legacies in your setting? Does it need to be begun? Might it be

explored more broadly? Are there legacies from which your community has already benefited? Any cautions?

3. Perhaps your conversation might be enriched by Roland Martinson's suggestion of a "spark hunt" to affirm and discover one's passions and all the possible applications of that passion. He offers a series of thought questions to start the sparks:
   - "What have I *always wanted to do* but never had time to do?
   - What did I *used to enjoy* but have drifted away from?
   - What am I *really good at* and *enjoy doing?*
   - What am I *curious about?* What is something I might try? What is something I want to learn?
   - How do I *play?*"[10]

4. When I visit with older people about legacies, they tend to speak about the people in the family and the property and/or money they will leave them. What are your thoughts on expanding this conversation to broader views of legacy?

5. I have heard of a church that formed a "Legacy Fellowship." To be a part of it, persons designate a tithe—one-tenth—of their estate to the church and its ministries. How does this strike you? Does your community have anything like it? How would such a proposal be received where you live and serve?

6. What about your own passions and legacies? What do you hope your biggest contribution in life will be? What from among your interests would you like to see strengthened and perpetuated?

## NOTES

1. Quoted in Evan Esar (ed.), *20,000 Quips & Quotes: A Treasury of Witty Remarks, Comic Proverbs, Wisecracks, and Epigrams* (New York: Barnes & Noble Books, 1968), 475.

2. Martenson, *Elders Rising*, 117, 121.

3. Martinson, *Elders Rising*, 119–21.

4. Martinson, *Elders Rising*, 122.

5. Butler, *Why Survive?* , 415, 381.

6. Kevin Damask, "Ex-teacher's Property to be Auctioned Sat," *Columbia Journal*, reported in *Wisconsin State Journal*, October 23, 2019, A5.

7. Thomas Moore, *Ageless Soul: The Lifelong Journey Toward Meaning and Joy* (St. Martin's Press, 2017), 196.

8. Moore, *Ageless Soul*, 187.

9. Moore, *Ageless Soul*, 199, 200.

10. Mortenson, *Elders Rising*, 127.

*Chapter 9*

# Experience Spiritual Journeys and Growth with Us Elders

Listen to me, O house of Jacob . . . even to your old age, I am [God],
even when you turn gray, I will carry you.
I have made, and I will bear; I will carry and will save.

—Isaiah 46:3-4

Religion is not a topic, not a course, not simply a body of beliefs.
It is a process of becoming.

—Joan Chittister[1]

Does a person's spirituality deepen as one ages?

George Vaillant wondered about this. In his longitudinal studies of adults, he found the answer unclear. However, he did note that growing older does alter the conditions of life that are conducive to spirituality. He offered several examples, "Aging slows us down and gives us time to smell life's flowers. Aging simplifies our daily routine and facilitates the acceptance of the things we cannot change. Aging banks our instinctual fires and increases our capacity to be internally quiet. Aging compels us to contemplate death. . . . Aging focuses us toward becoming one with the ultimate ground of all being."[2]

This may mean that older people are no more spiritual/religious than others, but they do have more spiritual tasks to address or that lifelong spiritual tasks are becoming more urgent. It might be time to work on some spiritual concerns and interests that have been denied or ignored for too long. *The Dictionary of Pastoral Care and* Counseling notes that the theological issues of the aging include vocation, finitude, and the threat of nonbeing.[3] Big, threatening topics those! Parker Palmer puts it well, "If it's true, . . . that old is just another word for nothing left to lose, then taking the risk of a deep inward dive should get easier with age."[4]

Pastoral caregivers encounter a tremendous variety of ways older people engage this dimension of their lives. And the leaders will need to respond with care in a myriad of ways. In this book, other chapters speak *implicitly* of spirituality-spiritual growth—for example, our search for meaning, passions and legacy, preparing for dying, memorials after one dies, and more. In this chapter, we will explore *explicit* spiritual growth issues and aims.

## DIFFERENCES FROM THE PERSPECTIVE OF FAITH STRUCTURE

To begin, there are wide differences among older persons in the framework or structure of their faith.

James Fowler spoke of this as "Faith Development." In this regard, it is important to be clear that he spoke of the structure, not the content of one's faith and spirituality. Fowler conducted hundreds of interviews and came to a perspective on this evolving structure of people's faith. He believed that (a) this process was growing in complexity; (b) it is sequential in the stages that he identified and named; and that (c) it was invariant, happening in the same order for all persons. I have questions about his (c) assumption, but he offers us a starting place to explore lifelong spiritual journeys. Here then are the stages he identified:

Stage 1: Intuitive-Projective Faith (The Innocent).[5] This stage happens in preschool or early elementary years. It is a time when life is fantasy-filled. The child encounters new objects, experiences, and people, but faith is largely understood through the family experience.

Stage 2: Mythic-Literal Faith (The Literalist). In this stage, perhaps childhood, the person takes the beliefs, stories, observances, and moral rules found in one's faith and applies them all very literally. Symbols are seen as one dimensional and precise in meaning.

Stage 3: Synthetic-Conventional Faith (The Loyalist). This stage probably begins in adolescence and, like the others can continue for a lifetime. While a person can engage more complex values and information, it is mostly a conformist-belonging stage. The person views faith primarily in interpersonal ways. Belonging to a significant group is what is most important. There may be unquestioning loyalty to a leader. Anything that disturbs or disrupts one's close group or community of faith causes distress and is rejected.

Stage 4: Individuating-Reflexive Faith. (The Critic) may come in one's teens, twenties, thirties, forties, or—for some—never. In this stage, a person may begin to reject the family faith, church, and practices. The person struggles with new ideas and beliefs. It is not a comfortable stage, either for the person in it or for those who care about them. Some leave it as soon as possible, but others stay in it for a long time, maybe for a lifetime.

Those who describe their religious affiliation as "nones" may be in this stage. Persons disillusioned with a faith or a great movement—civil rights, for example—may reside here. A number of people may have what can be described as a "generic spirituality" not buying into any major religious group or system of belief. They may be here as well.

Stage 5: Conjunctive Faith. (The Seer) is a stage rarely experienced before one's thirties or forties. Here one integrates what one has experienced, learned, and discovered through the previous four stages and comes to an understanding of one's faith that is uniquely one's own. This person may reclaim some of the stories, teachings, and myths of one's heritage in a new way. There may be an understanding of paradox—the ability to unify opposites in mind and experience. There may also be a desire to know more about the beliefs and practices of other faiths. It may be a time of conviction, tolerance, and peace with what has been discovered and claimed.

Stage 6: Universalizing Faith (The Saint) is experienced by only a few rare individuals. Here the person has a vision of an ultimate environment that includes all being. The person may sense a call to incarnate and actualize an ideal that envisions an inclusive and fulfilled human community. Fowler commented that this was the stage that interested people the most and about which he knew least because there are so few of them. There are famous people who lived in this faith stage—Mahatma Gandhi, Thomas Merton, Clarence Jordan, Pope Francis, for example. There also may be such persons among those older adults with whom you minister. I have met a few in my ministry, and I am the richer for it.

What does this have to do with spiritual care of older adults? Those with whom we minister will be at many places in these journeys. There may be some who live in the comfort and joy of the faith they embraced as children and youths. The hymn "Tell me the Old Old Story" may express their faith. They hope their faith community is, as one church slogan put it "The end of your search for a friendly church." There are devout, faithful, generous people who stay in this part of faith development journey.

Others may be in a searching, criticizing, questioning, debating, and disillusioned phase of their faith journey. They may have been in that same place for years and show little inclination to change. And there may be a few that are the statesmen and stateswomen of the faith, those with whom you meet to strengthen and ground your own faith.

People live in the faith stage that is most comfortable to them, and they move on reluctantly and with great pain. They do so, only if that stage no longer meets their needs. Further, they don't see the whole picture as I have described it. At most, they see the next stage. Or, more probably, they only see that period in between these stages—of pain and unrest. This is when old answers no longer satisfy, new questions arise, and a new way of living faith is searched for but not yet seen.

And there may well be elders who live into dimensions of their faith that are well beyond where the caregiver is. We are wise to approach the spiritual journeys of elders with humility and openness to what we may learn or discover there. I remember a time when as a young pastor calling on a frail, dying, saint, I broke down and cried during my prayer for her. After I finished, she thanked me for the prayer but added that she knew times like this would come and she would be ok.

## SPECIFIC OPPORTUNITIES FOR SPIRITUAL GROWTH

### Spiritual Friend

What wisdom does information about faith development and spiritual growth offer us pastoral caregivers? I once heard this definition of friendship, "A friend is someone who accepts you and loves you totally and completely as you are—but still gently invites you to grow." As we pastoral caregivers live among older adults each with their varied journeys, we are called to be such spiritual friends, accepting, but aware of realms of growth possible for those who are open and willing to take the risk.

As a matter of fact, there is a long Christian tradition of care and guidance for the spiritual journey. It has been described as spiritual direction, spiritual mentoring, the Celtics' Anam Cara, or—my preferred terms—spiritual friend or holy friendship. Janet Ramsey's definition is helpful. Holy friendship, she says, "refer[s] to the spiritual intimacy through which persons are brought into close relationship with each other and with God. Holy friends share the belief that . . . their relationship is being held in God's loving care."[6]

What happens in such holy friendships? Aware that friendship cannot be imposed, the caregiver—lay or professional—will call or meet regularly, keep one's promises, and hold confidences in sacred trust. As friendship grows, there develops a sense of mutual giving and receiving. This may include shared memories and other confidences, prayer, forgiveness, and gratitude. Such friendships will be especially important with homebound persons but can be important to all. In Ramsey's essay that I just mentioned, she invites ministers to change their perspective in calling on "shut-ins" from ministry chore to a possibility of holy friendship.

The ministry person (again lay or professional) should not be surprised or discouraged if these friendships vary tremendously in how they are experienced, what is shared, and how close and deep the relationship becomes. This goes with ministry and with friendships.

## Disciplines and Practices

And so, some of the older adults in our care may be open to specific guidance in the ways that lead to spiritual growth. There are gifted authors who offer such guidance. Their usual words for these spiritual growth tasks are "practices" or "disciplines." Older people trying to stay healthy or regain health are well acquainted with the need for disciplines in the physical dimension of their lives.—exercise, diet, rest, and more.

And so these adults in our care may be open to the understanding that one's spiritual life is also strengthened by judiciously chosen, and regularly done "disciplines" or "practices" Dorothy Bass who has done much significant writing in this field notes, "Practices are those shared activities that address fundamental human needs and that, woven together, form a way of life."[7] Such practices may lead one to deeper harmony with one's higher power in life-enhancing ways.

Richard Foster, the author of *Celebration of Discipline,* writes, "God has given us the Disciplines of the spiritual life as a means of receiving his grace. The Disciplines allow us to place ourselves before God so that he can transform us."[8]

The practices-disciplines that people in your care find helpful may also be widely varied. Some may commit to group disciplines/practices such as faithful worship with a community or participating in a discussion or Bible study group. Or one may choose individual disciplines/practices, to sing, to pray, to meditate, to live simply, or to fast. Or perhaps the practice/discipline is to volunteer regularly at a soup kitchen or other service project.

Indeed, the richest of spiritual practices often combine something of the inner life (between one's soul and God) with an outer engagement of community life (between one's soul and the people and world that God created).

## Study and Conversation

When I asked religious leaders of older adults what spiritual growth efforts had the greatest response, I often heard of Bible study groups. These leaders experienced persons eager to find a fresh word or a new perspective from a Bible passage. They valued open-end conversation and being allowed to wander to where their study and thinking might take them. They appreciated a leader who trusted their questions and wisdom. A spirit of open-ended, shared, and mutual inquiry and discovery was what made this spiritual practice appealing. Both the Book and the group supported and strengthened their faith journey.

## Meditation and Contemplation

Many are also enriched when in addition to active praying, they supplement the prayer as talking with the practice of listening and waiting. In this type of prayer, sometimes called meditation or contemplation one may concentrate on a single phrase or word of scripture and remain there for some time,—perhaps fifteen minutes or thirty minutes. Perhaps a song or chant engages one's heart and mind. This can be so enriching, but it takes dedication to do it regularly and patience for oneself for how much wandering the mind does in the midst of it!

In turn, one might be drawn to Parker Palmer's broader concept of contemplation. Palmer says contemplation can be defined not by any particular form but by its function. *"[C]ontemplation is any way one has of penetrating illusion and touching reality."*[9]

He notes that there are persons who are "contemplatives by decision"— who regularly and faithfully do this day after day. And then there are "contemplatives by catastrophe." Palmer says that he is one of the latter. These persons turn to renewing disciplines when something untoward happens whether it is exterior (such as a fall or a sickness) or interior (such as depression or despair). He writes "My wake-up calls generally come after the wreck has happened and I'm trying to find a way to dig my way out of the debris."[10] Either way, contemplation is an open door to the healing one desires and needs.

This is a small smattering of the life-enriching disciplines/practices that are possible. Those who want to start on digging deeper may be enriched by either or both of two books, Dorothy Bass (ed), *Practicing Our Faith* and Richard Foster, *Celebration of Discipline.*

## MODEL, RECOGNIZE, AND ENCOURAGE GRATITUDE-GIVING THANKS

Another opportunity with the people in our care is to model and invite a deeper hold of gratitude, of thankfulness and to make it more a consistent part of a person's life. Mary Pipher so wisely counsels:

"Gratitude is a life skill that can be improved with practice. . . . Feeling grateful is not a moral injunction, but rather, a healthy habit that we can learn to employ with greater frequency."[11]

Robert Emmons, prominent researcher on this topic describes gratitude as "a felt sense of wonder, thankfulness, and appreciation for life." He speaks of three aspects of gratitude. For one, there is the perceptual aspect that notices with appreciation all that is good in life. Then there is also an intel-

> I did not ask for success. I asked for wonder. And you gave it to me.
>
> —Abraham Heschel

lectual aspect which recognizes that the goodness we experience comes from sources outside ourselves—other people, perhaps pets, perhaps God. And then there is an emotional aspect that values both the gift and the intentions of the giver, with the impact that we feel thanks, and perhaps even love.[12]

Pipher reminds us that often "gratitude doesn't correlate with circumstances," and, in this connection tells of Muriel and her mother. Muriel had flown to be with her mother in her last days. As she sat by her mother's bedside, she thought of her mother's long sad history. Her mother had been orphaned, worked as an unappreciated housekeeper, married an abusive man, lacked education, and so made her living by cleaning hotel rooms. As far as Muriel remembered, the only thing her mother had ever enjoyed was coming to her dance recitals.

One day, her mother "woke with a start. She put her hands on either side of Muriel's faced and pulled her in close—eye to eye. She told Muriel, 'I have had a wonderful life. Remember that.'"[13] After this she fell into a sleep and the next morning was gone.

Meister Eckhart once wrote, "If the only prayer you say in your life is 'thank you,' it would be enough."[14] Words of gratitude, both to those near at hand and to our source, is a spiritual task all can learn or improve. Modeling and encouraging gratitude is at the heart of spiritual ministry with persons of all ages, including older adults.

## FIND, AND HELP OTHERS FIND THEIR "THIN PLACES"

Another spiritual task that we can model and encourage is to give attention to one's life enhancers. These enhancers may be special places, or persons, or occasions, or times, things we do, or things that are done for us, or things that just are. The Celtic Christians speak of "thin places" where the veil between worlds is more transparent.

Though Mary Pipher does not use the term "thin places" she describes one of hers, the migration of Sandhill cranes along the Platte River in Nebraska. She writes,

> Every spring I celebrate by visiting Rowe Sanctuary and spending the evening in a blind along the Platte. The cranes land just after dark and form islands in

the silver river. The sky is filled with birds. Their calls blot out all other sounds. It seems as if the world were made of cranes.

Every year I experience the best crane year ever. That is because every year I feel wonder and we can't parse wonder. Present wonder seems the best only because it is happening in the moment.[15]

The questions you might ask yourself and those with whom you minister to elicit this may be "Where or when do you feel closest to God? When or where are you most filled with awe? What places or events are times of reunion with your faith?" It may help if you share your own. Mine would include the birth of a child, a sleeping child, a quiet starry night, a summer evening with fireflies, a pianist or organist beautifully playing a hymn arrangement or the privilege of playing beautiful music—with a band or by myself. I also think of certain conference places, Christian camps, retreat centers, where the natural beauty and the spiritual quests make them mystic—yes, thin places.

## BE AWARE OF THE SPIRITUAL DEPTH
## AND POWER OF MUSIC

YoYo Ma once wrote, "Think of the inner life—where the music starts."[16] While it is not exactly clear what he meant in this cryptic statement, he does point to another ministry opportunity for spiritual enrichment and growth—music.

Music has the power to touch parts of our brain and soul that may not be touched in any other way. Mel Williams, a self-described "singing minister," asks why singing is so important and reflects, "What I've concluded is that singing inspires hope. . . . Singing forms community. . . . When we sing, we can't do anything else. We get 'lost in wonder, love, and praise,' . . . Songs express blessing, forgiveness, delight, and lament." Williams often finds an old hymn popping up in him, and then, "the song is singing me."

He concludes his reflection, "Theologically, it seems clear to me that God has chosen music as a primary vehicle to reach us. God rides on music. Singing becomes a spiritual practice; it wakes us up and gives us a surge of hope."[17]

### Music Affirms Faith

There are several places where music may offer spiritual enhancement. One way is as a means to consolidate, celebrate, and reaffirm one's faith. Williams tells of times when persons would confide that they were unsure about what they actually believed. At such times, he would ask if they had favorite hymns. If so, he would tell them, "Make a list of your favorite hymns and you will see what you believe." When the mind is struggling or confused, hymns move us into what our hearts are saying. Our well-loved hymns become a storehouse and expression of our heritage, our faith, and our spiritual commitment.

It has been said that a person most loves the music that comes from the time when they fell in love. Likewise, older adults love the music from the time when they fell in love with the God of their faith, probably from their teens and twenties. An old-time hymn sing may be so rewarding and enriching for elderly people. Of course, what music this is will vary for each of the cohorts of older adults as well as the religious tradition in which they were raised.

Lorraine J., a friend of mine, suffered a stroke. She survived it for a few years but came out of it with her speech garbled. She just could not put a complete sentence together. However, each evening her husband Charles would come to the nursing home and sing hymns with her; she remembered and sang every word! Though some may have a scientific explanation for that, they found it so comforting and healing through the last months of her life.

## Music Touches Persons with Dementia

Another way music heals is in making contact with persons experiencing dementia. The documentary film "Alive Inside" records the remarkable impact of providing an MP3 with music of one's young adult years to persons with dementia. Withdrawn, passive people become alive, animated, remembering, and aware, at least for a time, more than they have been in years.

Shannon Henry Kleiber writes of her mother who has been in memory care for two years. Usually that is a rather quiet place. However, she was amazed when she visited a music event, "My mom, and others, were up and away from their walkers and wheelchairs, singing, dancing, swaying, and smiling."

"How could this be? I had a feeling that if people who were barely verbal or immobile a few minutes before could transform into this joyful bunch, anything would be possible." Later at a "drum circle," her mother sang every word of "You are My Sunshine," which, she said, she remembered her mother and father playing.

Kleiber learned that research on music therapy shows that music creates sensory stimulation in people with dementia. Further, it can be a nonmedical treatment option for anxiety and stress. Whatever the explanation, something wonderful was happening![18]

Singing or hearing the choruses, hymns, gospel songs from one's child-hood and youth often has a similar awakening and comforting effect to older folks suffering from dementia. Wonderful things happen when the gift of faith music from one's roots is re-experienced.

## Music Consoles the Dying

And again, music can be an important means of solace with a dying person. In this regard, Meganne Masko interviewed chaplains and music therapists about appropriate ways of offering music therapy as well as the impact of music with terminally ill patients. They agreed that the music provided should fit the religious heritage and journey of the patient as well as being culturally appropriate.

When these guidelines were followed they saw many important gifts for the patient—"music therapy could be used to assist with meditation, anxiety reduction, increasing socialization, facilitating emotional expression and transcendence, enhancing feelings of connection with a higher power, and increasing feelings of spiritual comfort."[19]

It is wonderful when a music therapist is available. If not, we can summon the music resources of our ministry and be present with reassuring music of the faith of the one dying as we are present in this spiritual step out of this life.

## OFFER SOLACE TO THE LONELY

Another spiritual ministry opportunity is to be present to persons' grieving and loneliness. By growing old elders have lived longer than some of the precious people in their lives. Quite probably they have had to move away from others, or friends have moved away from them. As Joan Chittister has written, "Aloneness is the new monastery of the elderly."[20]

Geriatrician Louise Aronson notes, "The health impact of social isolation is equivalent to smoking fifteen cigarettes a day. All else being medically equal, loneliness increases mortality by 26 percent."[21]

Yes, indeed, loneliness hurts! It is dangerous. As Aronson noted, it may be, that for some, loneliness kills. Therefore, an important ministry task is twofold: One task, as much as possible, is to surround the lonely with caring persons, including ourselves.

The other is to invite persons to turn loneliness into the practice of contemplation which can take many forms. This leads us to other aspects of the contemplation of which we spoke earlier. It may be seeing and entering into the beauty of nature or music. Contemplation may also be calling up memories to savor. Or, contemplation may be breathing deeply, sensing the world slowing down, and being alone with the Alone. Or contemplation may be holding up people and causes in ongoing prayer.

In this way it may be that one takes at least some of the biting loneliness of elder life and turns it into solitude. For solitude involves living with memories, reliving wondrous moments, communing with the One who was before us, after us, and with us.

## CONSIDER AGING ITSELF AS A
## SPIRITUAL GROWTH POSSIBILITY

What are other spiritual tasks in this life stage? And what are the resources to guide and strengthen people through them? For one, a person needs to learn to live with loss. What losses? The losses of a lifetime. Moving through life, one loses one's parents, then quite probably some other elders, contemporary friends, siblings, perhaps a life partner. Then one loses one's work. Along with that, there may be loss of dreams for one's life. And then one loses, first youthful and midlife vitality and then bodily functions—as we have mentioned, four out of five older adults have at least one chronic condition, and many have several. It is an important task throughout life, but especially for elders to learn to let go, and trust one's ultimate source to sustain through this journey.[22]

Moving through this time of life is different from anything older adults have experienced in earlier life stages. If they move beyond resistance and denial, there are delights and discoveries. However, these can only come to the open-minded and open-hearted aging person.

Eugene Bianchi spoke of old age itself as just such a time for personal development, a spiritual journey. And then he asked this piercing question about the various activities, components, and patterns usually associated with successful aging. "Do they foster *soul-making*, that is, the fullest expansion of the inner potentials of the elderly person?"[23] Older adults are led to ask, even as their physical bodies may be bending and shrinking and their physical strength waning, is their soul growing into the persons they have dreamed of becoming? Is soul-making happening in their inner selves and outer relationships?

Lars Tornstam, a Danish social scientist offered a fascinating new term to describe the life-enriching change that can happen in aging persons. His term is "gero-transcendence." Tornstam came to this concept when he did a study of 922 Danes over the age of seventy-five. He found that 75 percent of them perceived a growth in spirituality in themselves from their earlier life. They responded positively to such statements as "I have more delight in my inner world," and "The border between life and death is less striking," and "How unimportant an individual life is, compared to the continuation of life as such."[24]

Tornstam spoke of "a time of gero-transcendence in which individuals gradually experience a new understanding of fundamental existential questions—often a cosmic communion with the spirit of the universe and a redefinition of the self and relationships with others." He went on to say that this is a shift "from a materialistic and pragmatic view of the world to a more cosmic and transcendent one."[25] There is less interest in material things. Solitude became more attractive.

This awareness varied from person to person in his study. And it will differ with each of the persons with whom we minister. His careful study invites persons to ask, what are we discovering or experiencing when we quiet ourselves and listen within to that part of the life journey called aging?

To come at this from a different angle, Erik Erikson was a pioneering scholar who helped us realize that we grow and change throughout our lifetimes. After describing the developmental issues of children and youths, he went on to describe subsequent developmental issues for young adults, middle adults, and older adults.

The issue or task of later adulthood, Erikson believed, was integrity versus despair. The question is, can one come to the end of one's life with "ego integrity"—that is acceptance of responsibility for one's life? Can one see and believe that one's life had meaning and purpose? If one can give even a qualified "yes" to those questions, one comes to the end of life with integrity, if not with despair.[26] Erikson leads older adults to consider an important late-life question—What do I see and how do I feel as I reflect on my life journey, my growth, my work and contributions, my relationships? If only anger and regret come to mind, then I answer with despair. If one can accept the worth of one's self, one's life, one's contributions and relationships, then a person answers with integrity.

Elizabeth MacKinlay built on the insights of these scholars and took it further by explicitly exploring spiritual growth in the fourth age of life. As mentioned in chapter 1, the fourth age is the age of frailty, dependency, approaching life's end, and needing care. From careful and respectful listening to people in this stage of life, she concluded that the spiritual journey does not end when people age come to this time in their lives.

The spiritual tasks of this population, she discovered, included at least the following: finding intimacy both with God and with others; transcending the loss and disabilities that come to the person; finding hope; and also finding final meanings in response to ultimate meanings in life.[27] How these are addressed will vary with the religion, spirituality, culture of the older person. The individual personality of the older person and the grieving, pain, and suffering she or he is enduring will also affect how these final meanings are addressed—or avoided.

The types of questions she asked in her research may be helpful to us clergy and chaplains as we attempt to be in touch with persons in these final years, months, or days of their spiritual journeys. Here are some of those questions: "What makes your life worth living? Are there things that are hard for you now? What is hardest for you now? How do you cope with the difficult things in your life?" and "Where do you find what brings greatest meaning in your life? What do you think God is like? Is religion important to you? If yes, in what way is it important? Is your spiritual life important to you? If yes, in what way is it important? Do you go to church [or other place of worship]? If no, did you used to go? Which ways of engaging with life's meaning do you use and/ or would like to use?"[28] After that last question there are boxes the interviewer could check depending on what the person indicated. The boxes include "worship, prayer, reading of scripture, meditation, music, art, environment, other."[29]

There are more questions, growing in specificity. These provide an entry into guidance for those of us ministering with older adults. MacKinlay has discovered that focused care and attention can be of help to frail older adults in spiritual reminiscence and transcendence and can be of help in supporting frail elderly people in their dying process.

How I wish more could hear and believe Joan Chittister, to repeat the quote with which we began, "Religion is not a topic, not a course, not simply a body of beliefs. It is a process of becoming."

## FOR REFLECTING AND CONVERSING

1. As you think about the older adults with whom you minister, how would you describe the variety of spiritualities and spiritual journeys among them? What do they have in common spiritually?
2. At times in this chapter it is suggested that there are older adults among us to whom we may turn for greater spiritual wisdom and maturity than we, their ministers, have. Do any persons like this come to mind? What do/might they teach you? What would you like to say to them? To ask them?
3. Of the various ways mentioned in this chapter, what have been most helpful to you in touching older adults' spiritual hungers and journeys? What did this chapter miss?
4. Are there older adults who are giving spiritual leadership and care to your faith community? In what ways? Have you acknowledged that gift? Encouraged it?
5. What, if any, have been your experiences of music being spiritually enriching and touching the souls of older adults? When has music touched and enriched your soul?
6. From the brief description given, what of MacKinlay's views, methods, and questions would you like to use in ministering with people in the fourth age of life?

7. Read and reflect on the poem "Two Gods." What, if any, points of contact does it make with your ministry with older adults?

## NOTES

1. Chittister, *The Gift of Years*, 101.

2. Vaillant, *Aging Well*, 278.

3. "Older Persons, Pastoral Care and Counseling of," *Dictionary of Pastoral Care and Counseling, Expanded Edition* (Nashville: Abingdon Press, 1990, 2008), 808–10.

4. Palmer, *On the Brink of Everything*, 136.

5. This section is a brief summary of James Fowler, *Stages of Faith* (New York: Harper and Row, 1981). The parenthetical titles for each of the stages comes from Charles McCullough, *Head of Heaven, Feet of Clay* (Cleveland: The Pilgrim Press, 1981).

6. Janet L. Ramsey, "Holy Friendship: Reimaging Ministry with Homebound Older Adults," *Word & World* 26, no. 3 (Summer 2006): 259–68.

7. Dorothy Bass (ed.), *Practicing Our Faith*, 2nd ed. (San Francisco: Jossey-Bass, 1997, 2010), xi.

8. Richard Foster, *Celebration of Discipline* (San Francisco: HarperSanFrancisco, 1978, 1997). Capitalizing his.

9. Palmer, *On the Brink of Everything*, 57, italics his.

10. Palmer, *On the Brink of Everything*, 59.

11. Pipher, *Women Rowing North*, 161.

12. Robert A. Emmons, *Thanks! How the New Science of Gratitude Can Make You Happier* (Boston: Houghton Mifflin Company, 2007), 35, 30–55.

13. Pipher, *Women Rowing North*, 162–63.

14. Quoted in Emmons, *Thanks*, 90.

15. Pipher, *Women Rowing North*, 249–50.

16. Quoted in Vaillant, *Aging Well*, 257.

17. Mel Williams, "Singing Our Way to Hope," accessed November 15, 2019, https://faithandleadership.com/mel-williams-singing-our-way-hope.

18. Shannon Henry Kleiber, "The Power of Music and Memory: 'Music Was Waking Up Something Within Each of Them,'" accessed January 6, 2020, https://www.ttbook.org/interview/power-music-and-memory-music-was-waking-something-within-each-them.

19. Meganne K. Masko, "Music Therapy and Spiritual Care in End-of-Life: A Qualitative Inquiry into Ethics and Training Issues Identified by Chaplains and Music Therapists," *Journal of Music Therapy* 53, no. 4 (2016): 321.

20. Chittister, *The Gift of Years*, 104.

21. Aronson, *Elderhood*, 295.

22. R. Scott Sullender, *Losses in Later Life: A Way of Walking with God* (New York: Haworth Pastoral Press, 1999), Italics his.

23. Eugene Bianchi, *Aging as a Spiritual Journey* (Chestnut Ridge, NY: Crossroad, 1984), 196.

24. Summarized and quoted in Vaillant, *Aging Well*, 278.

25. Lars Tornstam, "Gerotranscendence in a Broad Cross-Sectional Perspective," *Journal of Aging and Identity* 2, no. 1 (1977) as quoted in Elizabeth MacKinlay, James Ellor and Stephen Pickard (eds.), *Aging, Spirituality, and Pastoral Care: A Multi-National Perspective* (New York: Haworth Pastoral Press, 2001), 36.

26. Erik Erikson, *Childhood and Society* (New York: W.W. Norton and Company, 1950), 147–53.

27. MacKinlay, *Spiritual Growth*, 23–25.

28. MacKinlay, *Spiritual Growth*, 246–49.

29. MacKinlay, *Spiritual Growth*, 249.

# Two Gods

## I

A boy was born 'mid little things,
    Between a little world and sky—
And dreamed not of the cosmic things
    Round which the circling planets fly.

He lived in little works and thoughts,
    Where little ventures grow and plod
And paced and ploughed his little plots,
    And prayed unto his little God.

But as the mighty system grew,
    His faith grew faint with many scars;
The Cosmos widened in his view—
    But God was lost among His stars.

## II

Another boy in lowly days,
    As he, to little things was born,
But gathered lore in woodland ways
    And from the glory of the morn.

As wider skies broke on his view,
    God greatened in his growing mind;
Each year he dreamed his God anew,
    And left his older God behind.

He saw the boundless scheme dilate,
    In star and blossom, sky and clod;
And as the universe grew great,
    He dreamed for it a greater God.

Sam Walter Foss, 1858–1911 found in *Masterpieces of Religious Verse* and in the Common Domain.

# Chapter 10

# Remember the Doing in the Caring

Do not neglect to show hospitality to strangers, for by doing that some have entertained angels without knowing it.

—Hebrews 13:2

In this chapter, we again change pace. While our focus has been on ministry in the face of the major issues that elders experience, here, the accent will be on acts of kindness. Such acts are mostly small, but they touch another's life, enrich it, and perhaps, banish or reduce the loneliness, at least for a while. Some of these are deeds that older adults provide for each other. They may also be caring acts from younger to older, or for that matter older to younger.

Consider these a brainstorm to stimulate thinking about other possible caring gifts. Here are some observations and thoughts to stir your recognition and creativity in making a more beautiful world for all of us.

Before I go on to those suggestions, a word of perspective. As mentioned earlier, I wrote most of this chapter well before the COVID-19 pandemic. I am editing and polishing it in April 2020, while the stay-at-home and social-distancing orders are at their heights. As long as this is true, the parts about face-to-face human contact must be delayed. Other parts are out of touch with my present reality. This chapter asks of you an extra effort of translating pre- and during-pandemic needs and opportunities to post-pandemic ones.

I do not know when you will see this, but clearly it will be at a different time in our twenty-first-century history than I am writing. So, I urge you, take what is helpful as you read it, and rewrite-rethink the rest. At the end of this book, I will provide a postscript chapter on ministry with older adults after the pandemic.

## TRANSPORTATION

There are many ways a gift of a ride can ease a problem or open up an adventure.

Rides to medical appointments can be so helpful. I recall a time when an older man, Charles needed to have a series of radiation treatments on consecutive days. A younger friend contacted several people willing to help, arranged a schedule from their availability, and sent out the schedule to all involved. And so, Charles made it to his appointments, on time, every day.

For some of us elders, it is hard to ask for what we want or need. And so, offers of rides to worship or other church events, occasional or regular may be a welcome gift. Letting an older adult know that it is always ok to call and ask for a ride is helpful so that we do not have to worry about being a burden or nuisance.

Some may have an additional need. Along with the ride, they may need a companion for their visit to doctor, dentist, pharmacy, grocery store. As previously mentioned, they may need an extra set of ears with medical people, or someone to help them get their purchased goods to the car and into their home.

During the pandemic, many stores developed delivery services—groceries and more would be brought to the one purchasing them. Possibly some of these services will remain in place.

While transportation is a frequent need, some creative souls find a way to answer their need for human contact and friendship in other ways. I am aware of two older adults, one with brittle diabetes and many complications, the other blind. They called each other every morning and did the crossword puzzle together over the phone. And they did this for a number of years.

## PETS

Many older people have had pets for all or much of their lives. When the time comes to move into a smaller and safer housing, an urgent question may be, "Can I bring my pet with me?" These well-loved animals have become part of the family, and so the need to leave them behind may feel cruel indeed. The community where I live allows pets, subject to certain policies, and restrictions. I am told by some of the pet owners that they would not have come here if their pet was not allowed to come with them.

This leads to two different kinds of acts of kindness. For one, a person can take one's pet to visit with persons. There are a number of animals that can be helpful. However, in this brief description, I will concentrate on dogs. What is a "therapy dog"? A Wikipedia article answers—"A therapy dog is a dog that is trained to provide affection, comfort and support to people in hospitals, retirement homes, nursing homes, schools, libraries, hospices and/or disaster areas."[1] This may be an informal description for a person's well-trained dog, or more formally for one trained and evaluated by a national organization such as the Alliance of Therapy Dogs.[2]

Involving animals in offering care goes back at least to Florence Nightingale who discovered that patients living in a psychiatric institution were relieved from anxiety when they were able to spend time with small animals. Sigmund Freud also engaged animals in treatment—he discovered that some patients found it easier to talk to his dog than to him.

Before being allowed in an institution, a dog must have had all its shots—Rabies, Distemper, Bordetella. It must be trained to be friendly, not boisterous, calm, comfortable with people with many different issues, and open to touch and petting. For years, Sharon took her small lap dog, Lilly, a Jack Russell Terrier on countless visits. Lilly was everyone's friend,—many of us mourned when, old and feeble, she had to be put down. Sharon is now continuing her therapy dog visits with Prissy, a Chiwawa-Rat Terrier mix, a rescue dog that she adopted, cared for, and trained.

Some of those she visits just want them to walk by where they can be seen. Others want to pet, touch, perhaps hold, and spend a few minutes with the dog. Occasionally, people will begin to talk about their memories of their dogs or other pets. There is one woman, confined to her bed who wants Prissy up on the bed with her for a little visit and cuddle. Sharon observes "We just come, we don't have to do anything but be there and available, and we help people feel happy."

Acts of caring can come from pet and owner, but sometimes acts of caring need to be offered to them as well. Owners testify that pets are good for you. They keep you moving and stimulate you to think of someone other than yourself. But of course, the pet needs lots of attention, exercise, shots, medicine. One must always keep the pet in mind and provide for its care. And so, if a pet owner wants to travel or has health issues that need hospitalization, owner and pet are in need of help from others.

A woman who had a much-beloved cat needed to go and stay several days for rehabilitation treatments. Her group of friends rallied around her. They set up a schedule for each of the friends to have a "cat day,"—that is, going to their friend's apartment, be sure the cat had food and water, and spend some time with the cat. Others have taken a friend's dog out for a walk on a day when it was helpful and needed. There are rich opportunities for caring from pets and their owners; there are also rich opportunities for offering caring to pets and their owners.

## CHILDREN

If my small sample is representative, older adults show more pictures of the infants and children in their lives than any other subject.

In many older adult facilities including where I reside, children are rarely seen. Whenever people with small children come to visit, older adults perk up and take notice. There are extra glances. Some admire from a distance, but others approach with smiles and words, hoping to get a response from the child.

And so, an activity that will be much appreciated is to bring children into contact with older adults. This can be for a one time, or occasional time. When my children were small, I would sometimes take one of them with me when calling on homebound older adults. For some who were quite withdrawn into themselves, a child's presence seemed to stimulate them and draw them out of themselves, at least for a little while. They might want to find a small treat or something interesting to show the child. My youngest child, Laurie, would make little cards or drawings to take as gifts to the persons we visited. I remember one time especially. When Laurie presented her drawing to "Helen," she responded with a great big thank you and then asked Laurie to tell her in detail how she made it. It was so affirming for Laurie, that once in a while I would see her at work and ask what she was doing. She would tell me she was making more pictures because "it's time for us to go see the old people again."

In a time like this, when increasing numbers of older adults have no grandchildren, or their grandchildren live at a distance and are rarely seen, a caring church leader might initiate a "Foster grandparent" program. Mary Pipher tells of visiting such a program in an inner-city school, where an older couple, the Murrows came to the school twice a week to work with two groups of third graders. The coordinator assigned them to children who had difficult home situations and could use a little extra TLC. They faithfully came, listened to their "grandchild" read, or helped prepare a report, with much encouragement and praise. They obtained permission from the coordinator to give the children Easter candy treats and to send them postcards when they were absent for a time on a trip. Pipher observed deep friendship and enthusiasm for each other as they helped the children work on their projects and talked about whatever came to mind. The child had an adult's full attention and encouragement, and even more, care and friendship.[3]

The foster grandparents experience could be brought into the life of a church. It could be quite simple, inquiring of young families if they would like such an older friend, and of older adults who would be willing. A little information on guidelines, and possible activities, with an occasional check-in has a strong possibility of making a small dent in the isolation that both older adults and younger families sometimes experience.

Another possibility is for a small group of older adults and a small group of children meet together, perhaps for a few times. They might do a shared storytelling time, sharing with each other about favorite games and activities (when the olders were children). Or they might do a simple craft project together. (In chapter 13, there will be a story of children creating a game to get to know older adults better.) Something that can make it extra special is to have each older adult paired with a specific child, and they continue their relationship with each other each time they meet.

I remember a one-time event of this kind. A regularly meeting older adult group invited the children's choir to come, sing for them, and then stay for lunch. The plan was to have a few children and a few adults at each table. The children enjoyed singing and the adults responded enthusiastically. However, the meal plan did not work very well. The children did not want to talk much, ate quickly, and rush off to be with the other children.

But then, it occurred to the children that the table decorations were foil-covered chocolate candies. And, maybe if they asked, the adults would give them some. The children started racing from table to table to try this out. The adults quickly caught on, and doled out the candy in exchange for an answer to one question, such as—what is your name? Who are your parents? Do you have any brothers or sisters? What is your favorite subject at school or your favorite game? This went on for quite a while until the candy was gone, and both adults and children were laughing and enjoying each other. This was just what those who planned the event hoped. It simply happened in a different way than they expected!

## FOOD

There has been a practice at the retirement community where I live that can be experienced in other places. People can request a small garden plot, perhaps a five by ten-foot plot in the ground, or a smaller one in a waist-high above-ground container. Most of us plant more than we can eat—especially if it is a good year. Very few of us preserve the abundance; rather we give it away. There are baskets on a table in the commons area of residences where the abundance may be left for anyone who would like it. Or we may simply give it away to people we see as we walk back from our garden. On several occasions, I have started back with a small bag of tomatoes and reached my apartment with none (to my wife's relief—the refrigerator was full of the yield from earlier days). Or I might offer a fellow gardener a tomato or a pepper and be given a handful of green beans in exchange.

Caring through food can take many forms. Churches and other communities sometimes have a way for different persons to deliver a home-cooked meal to persons for several days after someone has returned home from a hospitalization or other health crisis. If they are caring for a single individual rather than a couple or family, the food is packaged in single-serving sizes to be used as needed. Gift cards to grocery stores may be a welcome gift for persons who may have both health and financial issues.

## RESPITE CARE—RELIEF FOR CAREGIVERS

In her book *Working Daughter*, Liz O'Donnell tells of simultaneously dealing with the health crises of her mother and father—differing, but both acute—while also employed in a demanding job. At almost exactly the same time, her mother was diagnosed with ovarian cancer and needed to be moved from her home to assisted living, and her father was in need of a safe place as his dementia worsened. Caring for them, finding appropriate facilities, negotiating their stays, filling out the paperwork nearly overwhelmed her. She wrote, "For the next few weeks my life was hell. Nights were a mix of bad dreams and insomnia. In the morning . . . I would consult my Excel spreadsheet that listed everything I needed to do for my parents. At its peak, the list had 196 items."[4]

Her acute stage—of facing these health crises and getting both parents the care and facilities they needed—lasted about six months. However, her caregiving responsibilities continued for years. She notes, "The average duration of a caregiver's role is 4.6 years, longer by 1 to 4 years for those caring for Alzheimer's and dementia patients."[5] She further notes that on average, a caregiver will spend 24.4 hours a week providing this care, although a third of caregivers provide 41 or more hours of care each week. Some of these caregivers are also employed outside the home.

Amy Ziettlow further points out that approximately 41.3 million Americans provide unpaid elder care. These caregivers, many of whom are also employed, not only spend hours a day on this care, but, according to a 2016 AARP survey, spend as much as $7,000 a year on out-of-pocket expenses related to caregiving.

Ziettlow identifies three different trajectories of caregiving with older adults—the roller coaster, the marathon, and the deep end. The roller coaster, she notes, "is a long-term period of support that requires intermittent periods of acute care." On the other hand, the deep end "is a short-term period of support that requires constant, on-site acute care." Her third category, the marathon "is a long-term period of continual support."[6]

The particularity of the needs of caregivers includes both personal support and more sensitive public policies. We will concentrate on the personal care, for now.

It is important to note that when offering pastoral presence and care with frail aging persons, it is equally important to also be attentive to the caregiver. How is that person doing? What would be helpful to support that person's life and efforts?

Time and again, I have heard family caregivers speak so gratefully of someone providing relief, even for an hour or two. For example, two or three older men would pick up their buddy who was confined to home, take him for a drive, stop, and eat lunch in a restaurant or have an ice cream cone treat. The men enjoyed each other, and his caregiving wife had two to three hours to rest or to do a few errands without worrying.

While occasional or spontaneous events like this are appreciated, such care is even better if regular and if it can be counted on. Discovering what the home caregiver would find most helpful and mobilizing people of goodwill to provide that support will literally be a Godsend. One of our neighbors has a plaque that says, "Friends are God's way of caring."

This can take many forms from one on one to larger group programs. The Older Adult Ministry of First United Methodist Church of Corpus Christi, Texas has researched and developed a broad systematic approach, "The Oasis: A Caregiver's Day Out Ministry."

From their material—

"The OASIS Offers:

- Once per month (third Friday) respite program for people with Alzheimer's disease (AD) and other similar dementias who are being cared for at home by family members.
- It provides a chance to socialize in a warm and loving atmosphere.
- Offers the caregiver four hours of stress-free time to attend to their own personal needs.
- Is offered as a ministry to the community by First United Methodist Church of Corpus Christi, TX in gratitude for God's many blessings. It is offered *free of charge.*"

Their further literature mentions that the only requirements are that the persons cared for must be continent and able to care for their bathroom needs as well as to be mobile. Using a walker is fine.[7]

## HOSPITALITY

One Valentine's Day when we called Mary Ann's grandmother, we could tell by the tone of her voice that something incredibly special had happened. Her young pastor and his wife had called her and several other widowed or single women in the church and said they wanted to have some people they loved in their home on Valentine's Day. The clergy couple hosted these several women for a simple Valentine lunch and dessert. We could tell from her description that this was an event to remember and to treasure.

In the family where I grew up, it was a custom at every holiday to look for people who would otherwise be alone and invite them to our festive holiday meal—Thanksgiving, Christmas, New Years. It was a custom we continued as adults with our family and community. Some elders were hesitant to accept this invitation, fearful they were invading sacred family time. We would reassure them that this was part of our family's tradition and the holiday would not be complete without them. As I look back on those experiences, I feel sure that we mutually enriched each other's holiday.

## ARTFUL VISITS

Perhaps the only time people call to share music is caroling at Christmas time. However, there are many other opportunities where bringing the arts to a lonely and isolated person can be so rich. Perhaps the caller can bring someone with a solo voice to sing selections, maybe some songs of the visited person's own choosing, can bring a moment of tenderness. A vocal trio or quartet can come to an individual or community and brighten many a day. Quiet instruments—harp, violin, guitar, cello and others, or other instruments played quietly may enhance the time with a person, and perhaps the neighbors.

Hannah Rosell found another way—she is a gifted artist. She would call on a person, visit and learn about their life, interests, past activities, then draw a picture that would include some of the things discovered, and leave it with them.

## HELPING HANDS—PHYSICAL LABOR

As Mary Ann and I lived in our free-standing home into our eighties, there were times when we were overwhelmed. Sometimes this happened with the ongoing care of home and yard. More often, it was urgent at emergency times, such as a flooded basement or a storm that tore branches off trees, filling our back yard with all sorts of debris. There were two times when a volunteer from our church appeared with his chain saw, and in an hour or two had cut up the largest of the felled limbs, tied up or bagged much debris and had it on the curb for pickup. We were so grateful.

In addition to emergency times, the home where older adults live will have wear and tear as well as cleaning needs that become more difficult with age.

We were so fortunate that for several years, our son-in-law John would spend a week of his vacation with us, doing whatever needed to be done, washing windows, repairing-painting fences, power washing cement floors and driveways, and much more.

Those with a knack for home maintaining skills can band together and offer simple home repair-maintenance services to people who are older or handicapped and cannot do the home care they once did. They may want to list the sorts of things where they can help, perhaps small painting projects, changing light bulbs, mowing lawns, simple carpentry, etc.

## HELPING HANDS—PAPERWORK

In a library near where I used to live, volunteers offered a vital service. On given days during tax season, there would be persons from AARP offering help with income tax forms. In addition to preparing tax reports, they would answer questions that puzzled those of us doing our own. And they would help locate those additional pages or schedules a person might need. It was so good to have a knowledgeable, caring resource person available during that often-stressful season. An older adult friend in another state told me that in response to her request, an AARP member came to her home and helped with her income tax. It was particularly helpful in that year of selling a home, moving, taking up residence in another state. All this can make for a complicated tax report!

Some older adults may need help—or someone to do it—as regards bills, payments, managing their financial affairs. Others may need to be sure that vital information—about access to financial accounts, lock boxes, or what they want done with their estate, large or small, after they die—is clearly communicated and in a safe place.

There are aspects of this that a discreet volunteer can assist. That person also needs to be aware when professional expertise is needed, and who are some of these professional people who are reasonable and open to working with the elderly and their issues.

## LEARNING, FELLOWSHIP, WORSHIP

The last seminary class I taught had twelve students, six in the room with me and the other six in five different states. The latter persons were engaging in "distance learning" by accessing a website with course materials and participating in the class through a software that makes such group meetings and exchanges possible.

With the pandemic bringing "Stay at Home" orders, churches suddenly faced the question of who they are when they could not assemble in one place. How can the contact, support, learning, worshipping functions happen when we are isolated from each other in our homes?

Churches looked for and found various technological platforms—that have been available for some time—to sustain their life, worship, and fellowship. There are webcasting platforms that are designed for passive consumption. Also, there are video conferencing platforms that allow all participants to be seen and heard. After the pandemic, these tools can be useful in helping older adults and other frail persons to be part of a community they treasure.

Each of these provides something of the ways a community of people can be in touch. Persons with technology skills could engage these various technologies and work it out with the people involved so that homebound persons might be able to "attend" their long-loved Church School Class or other group. I will say more about this in the postscript chapter.

During the stay at home order, there were also more familiar ways groups found to keep in touch—for example, by emails and phone calls. Our New Horizon band leaders would send all the band members on their email list a playful quiz with the promise of a hypothetical prize. For example, "Why did Beethoven start taking violin lessons at age 5?" Or "What do you get when all the band members have their masks in place?" And the various members responded with equally playful possible answers. It was great fun and compensated—at least a little—for not being able to be together for rehearsals and performances.

> I expect to pass through life but once. If therefore, there be any kindness I can show, or any good thing I can do to any fellow being, let me do it now, and not defer or neglect it, as I shall not pass this way again.
>
> —William Penn, 1644–1718

As I suggest this out of my teaching experience, I am aware of the many possible snafus due to poor connections, or antiquated computers. Those undertaking a ministry that uses technology need persons to teach how to access the group or worship service and possibly some funds to provide better equipment and connections when needed.

## SUPPORT IN TRANSITIONS

When the time comes to move from a home of many years into a much smaller apartment there is great stress. This includes deciding, selling, giving, what is not going to fit and selecting and moving what will. It is both exhausting and emotional.

With all the overwhelming tasks, it is easy to overlook another need. That is the need to say goodbye to a home, a neighborhood, a community where one has lived for years. In retrospect, I recall the wisdom of a friend. When they had moved their belongings to their retirement apartment but not yet released their house, he invited family and friends to a "house cooling" ceremony. He borrowed some folding chairs. Part of the time during that ceremony, they moved from room to room and shared memories of events that had happened in that room. With a prayer of thanksgiving for those years and trust for the future and light refreshments, they concluded the farewell to a home. He told me that doing this had helped him adjust more readily to his new apartment than would otherwise be true.

Caring friends can be of help in both the packing and hauling. They might also inquire about a "house cooling" time, and, if wanted, help with the celebration.

## AND SO

As I mentioned at the beginning of this chapter, much of it was written before the pandemic, and hopefully by the time you read this, the worst of that will be passed. None of us knows what the "new normal" will look like. Perhaps we will have learned some new ways and keep those practices in place. Possibly there will need to be permanent changes in the ways we relate and support each other. It may be that each religious leader will need to revisit and rewrite the thoughts here for a quite different time.

At any rate, this chapter has offered a few examples and brainstorming ideas about how love and care can be communicated. This is with the hope that whatever thoughts this generates will make the world of the older adults in your care, less lonely and more livable. When that happens—sensitivities increased, and caring acts expanded—my fellow older adults and I thank you.

## FOR YOUR REFLECTING AND CONVERSING

1. Where in this chapter did you identify activities you are already doing? How are they going? How could those activities be improved or enriched?
2. What ideas and examples in this chapter stirred an interest or curiosity for you? What should be your next step to investigate them? What did the chapter miss?

3. Who in your ministry—whether old or young—are most active in expressing care and support to those around them? How can they be affirmed? Encouraged? Invited into still other ways of expressing that care?
4. Apart and beyond this chapter, what are your best thoughts and strategies for communicating care with the older population in your community?

## NOTES

1. "Therapy Dog," accessed March 6, 2020, https://en.wikipedia.org/wiki/Therapy_dog.

2. "Caring People and Sweet Dogs," accessed April 17, 2020, https://www.therapydogs.com/.

3. Pipher, Another *Country*, 301–4.

4. O'Donnell, *Working Daughter*, 6.

5. O'Donnell, *Working Daughter*, 6.

6. Amy Ziettlow, "Journeys of Care: The Roller Coaster, the Marathon, and the Deep End," *Christian Century*, September 11, 2019, 10–11.

7. This information was found in a pdf booklet, "The Many Faces of Senior Ministries," from First United Methodist Church of Corpus Christi, Texas. I received this from Wayne DeHart following an interview with him, January 10, 2020.

## Chapter 11

# Prepare Yourself and Us
# to Say Goodbye

Even though I walk through the valley of the shadow of death, I will fear no evil for thou art with me.

—Psalm 23:4a RSV

To contemplate dying each day calls forth an instant reordering of priorities.
  Just like a quick and deliberate shake of a kaleidoscope,
  it creates a whole new patterning, a whole new view.

—Kathleen Dowling Singh[1]

We—all of us, young and old—live in a death-denying and death-ignoring culture. However, one of our ministry colleagues relates how he confronted this truth.

Matt Fitzgerald, a United Church of Christ minister, writes, "It feels ridiculous to say that a smartphone app changed my life. I'm not that shallow. But it happened."[2] He reflects on subscribing to an app called *WeCroak*. This app sends an alert to users five times a day at random times. The message is always the same. "Don't forget, you're going to die."

He recalls how this message came to him at various times—in the morning, drinking coffee, which he savored all the more; in the midst of an argument and power struggle with his son, which popped the conflict into perspective and calmed him; when listening to an extended critique of him by one of his parishioners, and allowed him to humbly listen. He reflected "I need more than the occasional reminder. . . . Five times a day feels right. . . . *WeCroak* named the object of my dread and sucked the threat right out of it."

He doesn't report on how this impacted his care of frail and dying people, but I would imagine there was a deep influence there as well.

The elders with whom we minister live in a life stage that differs from the others. Each of the other life stages has a transition into it and a transition out of it. For older adults, the transition into being an older adult may have happened in a number of ways—retirement, perhaps, or grandparenthood, or reduced strength and vigor, or a more severe health crisis. However, there is only one transition out of it—death. There are "You're going to die" reminders are all around us, in the frailty of our friends and family members, in our aching and weakening bodies, in the frequent funerals we attend.

So, elders who have tried to live life well have one more task—to die well. Psychologist Erik Erickson noted that one of the responsibilities of older adults who have aspired to live with integrity is to show younger generations not to fear death.[3] Of course, there is still death denial among older adults. We cannot force anyone to face death and take vital steps—we can only invite them. For, to die well requires moving beyond death denial to anticipatory thoughts, reflection, and actions. This in turn, has several aspects.

Surgeon Atul Gawande notes, "It is not death that the very old tell me they fear. It is what happens short of death—losing their hearing, their memory, their best friends, their way of life. As Felix put it to me, 'Old age is a continuous series of losses.' Philip Roth put it more bitterly in his novel *Everyman*: 'Old age is not a battle. Old age is a massacre.'"[4]

And so, along with the joy and inspiration of ministry with capable older adults, we also have a responsibility. That is to assist them as they think through and communicate their wishes that they may have as a good a death as possible. One vital part of this is discussing end-of-life issues.

Thinking and talking about end-of-life issues is so important, but so hard to do. Consider—"90 percent of people say they believe that talking with their loved ones about end-of-life care is important." However, "27 percent have actually done so." Further "60 percent . . . say making sure their family is not burdened by tough decisions is extremely important," but "56 percent have not communicated their end-of-life wishes." Further still, "80 percent . . . want to talk to their doctor about wishes for treatment toward the end of their life," but "7 percent have actually done that!" And "82 percent . . . say it's important to put their wishes in writing" but again, "23 percent have actually done it."[5]

A significant ministry is to encourage elders think through requests for their dying days and to help them communicate their wishes clearly to those entrusted with their care. And, of course, to be present with them when those days come.

## THE WHAT AND THE HOW OF
## END-OF-LIFE DECISIONS

There are three important and basic categories to include in the "What" for pastoral care as regards end-of-life decisions. One is to help people think through, determine, and discuss what treatments they want and what they do not want when in failing health. They need to discuss this both with their family members and with their healthcare providers. Second is to help people tend to their relationships that are most important to them, including estrangements or hurt feelings. The third is to invite people to claim, or re-claim, the resources of their religious faith in the closing chapter of their lives. To do each of these, elders will need to be invited to grow from death denial to wise preparation for it. I will explore each of these "what's" and then offer suggestions, and resources on how to provide these ministries.

### What—Aids in Discussing End-of-Life Medical Issues

(Throughout this section, I am going to explore the decisions an older adult will be wise to make. To do this, I will speak of a hypothetical older adult as "a person" and "they" or "their" as singular third-person pronouns as I describe the decisions "they" are wise to consider.)

This category—to make decisions about end of life and communicate about it—in turn, has three basic tasks: (a) to think through and state in writing, what a person would want and not want when the end of life is near; (b) to select and state the individual who will make sure their wishes are honored when they are no longer able to speak for their self; (c) to have a conversation with their physician or other health care provider and gain the health provider's support and cooperation for their end-of-life concerns. There also a couple of clarifications that might be helpful, one about palliative care and hospice, the other about euthanasia.

### (a) *Think through Requests for End of Life*

Here is guidance through these steps, mainly using one excellent resource *Caring Conversations: Making Your Healthcare Wishes Known*, published by the Center for Practical Bioethics, available free online.[6] Later, I will point you to other valuable resources. In the *Caring Conversation* resource, a helpful way into this important conversation is offered. The authors suggest engaging four basic questions:

"1. What concerns do you have about making decisions for yourself later in life?

2. What concerns do you have about your health and future health care?
3. Where do you want to receive care?
4. Who do you want to be with you? Who do you want to talk to?"

These questions are gentle but firm invitations to move beyond ignoring and denying to acknowledging that a person's limited life span will come to an end. From all they know from others' experiences and their own thinking and values, what will be important to them when they are close to death?

The next section of this booklet carries the conversation a step further by applying those values to questions about well-being and quality of life. If their health conditions change from the relative health they enjoy now, what that they now take for granted will be important? Who would be a person who want to stay near to visit? Will they want the ministries of a religious leader? If they can see, what reading materials or other objects would they like at hand? If they can hear, is there music or other sounds they would want to hear? What kind of music?

Then this guidebook takes yet another step. It describes three groups, and asks which one is most like them? The groups are:

- Group A: Some people say they only way they want to die, even if their condition is irreversible is with aggressive maximum medical intervention. (Do everything!)
- Group B: Some people say that aggressive intervention is fine but only for reversible conditions. If they were not getting better with a particular intervention, they would not want to continue it.
- Group C: Some people feel strongly that they do not want any form of artificial life support under any circumstances.[7]

Here is where the privileges and hazards of modern health care come into play. Most of us can remember a time when folks would say concerning an extremely sick loved one, "Do everything you can, Doc." Nowadays, that may not be a wise request, for there is so much that can be done. The question about some of these procedures might be, do they extend living, or do they extend dying? And do they bring additional pain and suffering? What is the quality of the life that may be kept functioning by "heroic methods?"

Some of these methods are awfully expensive, and this raises an issue not only for the individual family but about the resources of a nation. Richard Coble notes, "Over a quarter of all public health money, meaning Medicare and Medicaid, is spent on patients in the last month of life."[8] Worse yet, Dr. Angelo Volandes observes, "Americans receive some of the best health care money can buy; they also experience some of the worst deaths in the developed world."[9] Would they prefer fewer days lived with what quality of life they feel essential? Or would they rather have the doctors take every measure to extend life as long as possible, even though it may involve pain, discomfort, possibly unconsciousness? What is essential to feel life is worth living? While no one knows the exact circumstances they will face, it comes down to a question of whether one prefers Group A's answer or B or C.

Susan Block, a palliative care specialist tells of a difficult conversation she had with her own father as he faced surgery for a mass growing on the spinal cord of his neck. This was a procedure that had a 20 percent chance of leaving him quadriplegic. Hesitantly, she said to him, "I need to understand how much you're willing to go through to have a shot at being alive, and what level of being alive is tolerable to you." Her father responded, "Well, if I'm able to eat chocolate ice cream and watch football on TV, then I'm willing to stay alive." The answer shocked her,—her father was a distinguished professor emeritus, and she had never even seen him watch football.

However, he developed bleeding in the spinal cord and to save his life, the surgeons would have to go back in. This included an even greater risk of paralysis. They asked her what they should do. She recalled her father's answer. When the doctors said he would be able to eat chocolate ice cream and watch football, she said go ahead. Her father survived, gradually gained the ability to walk a bit, and had some productive years after that surgery.[10]

The *Caring Conversation* guide goes on to raise questions about some specific procedures. About breathing, "How do you feel about mechanical assistance to breathe?" And in regard to eating and drinking, what is acceptable to you and what is not when you are unable to take nourishment as you did when healthy?[11] The step of helping persons answer as clearly as possible about these difficult questions is important. Granted, these are always tentative answers for it cannot be known all the questions and treatments to be considered as a life nears its conclusion.

After answering these difficult questions there is another important step. That is to state these decisions, choices, and preferences in writing, to tell key family members about it, and to see to it that this information is available for those who will be responsible for this person's care. This statement is variously called an Advanced Directive, a Health Treatment Directive, or a Living Will. The *Caring Conversations* booklet provides a sample with some blanks to fill in one's own preferences.

(b) *Select and State the One Who Will Make Sure this Person's Wishes Are Honored*

An important next step is to select an individual they have chosen to make healthcare decisions for this person when they are no longer able to do so.

That is, choosing one who will accept the responsibility of being this person's health care power of attorney. Since this one may need to make decisions to cease treatment that they think the person would not want, the one selected should be deeply trusted and informed about what a person would want or not want if their health condition became extreme.

This may be a member of one's own family, or a friend, or someone whose wisdom and perspective they admire. Many health providers strongly advise against naming a group of persons (e.g., siblings) with this designation. The one chosen can, of course, consult with others, but the one designated should make decisions needed—in accord with the sick person's wishes as best they understand them. It is possible to change the one chosen for this role as life circumstances may change.

The one designated for this role is known variously as "health care proxy," "health care surrogate," "durable power of attorney for health care," or something similar.

Dr. Angelo Volandes suggests some probing questions to help a person select the best possible health care proxy.

1. Does your proxy understand what your values and priorities are? Do you trust your proxy with your life?2.Will your proxy be able to separate his or her feelings from yours and act on your wishes? 3. Will your proxy be a strong advocate of your expressed choices even if others—including your family members—disagree?4.Does your proxy live near you and will he or she be available when you need help them most?[12]

Once a choice is made and that person has agreed to serve, it should be written down in a document often called "durable power of attorney for health care" and carried—along with one's "living will"—every time they go to a hospital or on a trip. Some states require that these documents be notarized by a notary public. The *Caring Conversation* workbook provides a sample document for this purpose.

(c) *Have a Conversation with Their Physician or Other Health Care Provider*

A third important step—that so many intend but so few do—is to speak with one's physician or other health care provider about what a person is saying in their health care directive and designation of a health care proxy. It will be wise to make an appointment, stating the purpose of having this conversation. Or if there is already an appointment pending, to notify that time for this conversation is also requested.

It will be wise to ask the doctor for a POLST (Physician Orders for Life-Sustaining Treatment) or, depending on the state, a MOLST (Medical

Orders . . .) that authorizes the treatments and limitations discussed. Dr. Volandes notes that Advance Directives, and Designation of Health Care Proxy are legal documents, that simply "provide legal guidance and do not apply to emergency medical personnel." On the other hand, a POLST or MOLST is a Physician's order and will be implemented.[13]

### (d) *Clarification: An Important Distinction—Palliative Care and Hospice*

There is often confusion about palliative care and hospice. When pondering these end-of-life topics, it is important to know about palliative care and hospice and the distinctions between them.

Palliative care is a medical speciality which "focuses primarily on relieving suffering and improving function, not on curing illness."[14] It may also be designated as pain management, symptom management, or comfort care. Palliative care may be engaged while still working with medical staff in fighting one's illness. As Katy Butler describes it, their key question is "what matters to you?" and help you achieve it. She notes, "They also step in as truth-tellers, counselors and medical-decision coaches when other doctors feel unequipped to play these roles. They are not afraid to talk frankly about the realities of death and disability, and to help you prepare for them emotionally and practically." Because they "focus on the needs of the whole person, they often save people from falling through the cracks in fragmented health systems."[15]

On the other hand, hospice is a program, fully funded by Medicare, Medicaid, and some insurance companies, that requires *only* palliative care be utilized. Persons are admitted into this program with an admissible diagnosis and a reasonable prognosis of six months or less to live. Hospice provides invaluable support and care to terminally ill persons and their families. A team that includes doctors, nurses, social workers, and chaplains visits and offers support to the ill person and the family. Whatever of medical supplies that are needed is provided. A frequent lament is that people come into hospice too late, just a week or so before death, when the support over the months would have been so helpful. Both palliative care and hospice focus on the quality of life, the well-being of the patient, attentiveness to what is important to the patient as life comes to a conclusion.

### (e) *Clarification: Euthanasia*

When we consider what is wanted or not when seriously and terminally ill, the possibility of euthanasia may arise in the conversation. Legal euthanasia,—doctor-assisted suicide—is available in many countries in the world and in several states in our country. Extreme cases of horrible and incurable suffering may occasion discussion of this option.

For many of us, the difference between "active euthanasia" (administering drugs to end life) and "passive euthanasia" (refusing certain treatment options that would extend dying) is important and basic. When the quality of life is deteriorating, any patient and family should be able to say, "enough is enough" and to discontinue the life-death extending treatments. Quite possibly, the hospice alternative would be adequate.

## What—Helping People Leave with Relationships Healed or Healing

A second concern—equally important—is to reflect on what is unfinished in one's life. In particular, it may be good to consider what relationships are strained or broken and what life commitments are not yet fulfilled.

Matthew O'Reilly, an emergency medical technician, has attended to many people when they were dying. He saw much calm among these patients when notified they were dying. And then he added, "But most people have three pieces of unfinished business. They have regrets and want to be forgiven. They fear they'll be forgotten and hope they'll be remembered. And they want to know that their lives had meaning."[16]

In this regard, pioneering hospice doctor Ira Byock noted that the dying have five basic but important tasks. These are five conversations, five things to consider, say, and act. They are: forgive me; I forgive you; thank you; I love you; and goodbye.[17]

In regard to these five conversations, Donna Schaper wisely notes, "The good news is that you can start saying the first four anytime. And the even better news is that you can add a discussion of the next [goodbye] to any conversation, whenever you choose to do so."[18]

I have come to believe that the great wisdom in these five tasks applies not only to one's last months of life but to many other areas of relationship as well. Of course, as Schaper noted, the first four can/should often be spoken to keep relationships current and real. Further, one might want to express these thoughts when leaving a community to move to another. These are also good things to consider when retiring from a job or career. I engaged these questions in my seminary teaching when I was having a final class session with students who would soon graduate. Further, when I finished my time and was leaving a pastorate, I tried to bring these five statements into my farewell conversations with a congregation I had loved. In short, this can be part of a wholesome and healing philosophy of life.

Further still, these are good topics for older adults who are in reasonably good health and may be a few or several years from dying. Just as they have quite possibly have given away many possessions of a lifetime and live in smaller surroundings with simpler furnishings, they may want to do more "house cleaning." That is to take one's relational pulse, ask how they are doing in their most important relationships and basic commitments. Then they may want to make any needed decisions, conversations, or statements for that time of their lives.

But when the diagnoses and signs are that our life is ending, it becomes even more urgent to do and say what we need to conclude our life in the best possible way. It may be time for persons to say and hear:

- *Please forgive me* for my failings with you large and small. I may have been insensitive to your feelings and thoughts. I may have ignored questions you wanted us to discuss. I may have been busy with others when you needed me. I may have hurt you. And . . . For what I have done and what I have not done, please forgive me.
- *I forgive you.* I may have had frustrations and disagreements with you. These may have led to grudges between us. I may have thought my needs, ideas, and priorities were overrun. None of this seems so important now. I do not want any of these to be between us. And . . . I forgive you.

As regards this forgiveness asked for and offered, Joan Chittister's wisdom guides, "Only forgiveness is the therapy of old age that wipes the slate clean, that heals as it embraces . . . . Forgiveness puts life back together again. It is proof of our own learnings. It is sign of our own inner healing. It is a mark of our own self-knowledge. It is the measure of the divine in us."[19]

If the hurt is so huge as to make forgiveness seem impossible, perhaps at least compassion for the other may flow in the closing days of a life.

- *Thank you.* You have such an important place in my life. There are so many things you do without being asked and without being acknowledged. Thank you for your concern for my best welfare even when I did not recognize it. Thank you for being here now in these days of conclusion. And . . . Thank you.
- *I love you.* Through the years we have known each other, I have grown in my admiration, my respect, yes, my love for you. Perhaps we have known of the love between us without speaking of it. We might have worried about being misunderstood. But as I look back on my life, one of the things I most treasure is what we mean to each other. And . . . I love you.
- And *Goodbye.* With gratitude for you, with love and forgiveness, and clean clear air between us, goodbye. Let there be no regrets. We did our best. For our experiences, relationship, and memories, goodbye.

A person may need to do such a conversation with one, or few, or many. The conversation may take place in brief snippets, interrupted by others, or fatigue or, perhaps, the need for time before they can go on. Quite likely, they will never feel entirely complete. But how much better to try and come as far as humanly possible.

Some may think of different topics they would like to discuss with the people near to them, and to talk in a quite different way. All to the good. The important part is to be as healed and healing as possible in the important relationships of life as it nears its end. While this is important for oneself, it is also important as one shows those who come after us how to die well.

While working on this book, I experienced grief in my family. My only sibling, my big sister Ruth died. As I travelled to be with family as we mourned her death and celebrated her life, I became aware of another truth about these five statements.—You can say them after a person dies as well. After death, the survivors may have unresolved feelings and issues. To explore and say what needs to be said may be necessary for healing grief to happen. We, religious caregivers, are wise to be aware and available to people who may have this need following the death of a family member or friend.

*An Aside*

In all this end of life reflecting and living with imminent death, is there any room for humor? That, of course, is for the person in that end-of-life circumstance to answer. I am aware of a study by Dr. Kay Ann Herth, where she interviewed fourteen patients with a prognosis of six months or less to live. When she asked them about humor, 85 percent thought humor would be helpful, but only 14 percent experienced any humor. She heard such comments as "I try to be playful, but others won't respond." "If I ever needed humor it is now." "I want to smile and laugh, but that upsets my family."

She noted several contributions of humor for these terminal patients: For one, humor helped a patient's self-esteem. It was good to feel like a person out of sharing something positive. For another humor altered the patient's own attitude, to see things more positively and to put a new light on their situation. Further humor aided a patient's communication. It opened the door to ask questions that they might not have asked otherwise as well as to hear instructions they might have been too anxious to hear.[20]

## What—Claiming Religious and Spiritual Resources at the End of Life

Third, when approaching the end of our life, there is a need to claim the teachings, perspective, and consolations of one's religion or spirituality. As their religious professional, I need to be present and supportive of the dying patient's religion-faith-spirituality, not my own. I come with my heritage and beliefs and make them available when asked. Then I bear witness to the faith in which I stand.

Many years ago, I was worshipping in a Good Friday community service. A minister was speaking about Jesus's word in Luke 23:46. "Then Jesus, crying with a loud voice, said 'Father, into your hands I commit my spirit.'"

The pastor said that Jesus was showing us what death is. It is "Father, into your hands I commit my spirit." Further, Jesus showed us how to die. It is, "Father, into your hands I commit my spirit." Over the centuries, many have died with this prayer on their lips—Stephen (in Acts7:59), Thomas Becket, and Martin Luther, to name a few.

We can do well at the end of each day to offer this as our last prayer before we sleep, "Father into your hands I commit my spirit," In so doing we prepare ourselves for that day when we may pray it one last time in this life. We will speak more of this in the next chapter.

One's faith may be expressed in a fitting worshipful atmosphere while dying. Whatever rituals, practices, or objects that have been sacred to the person can be brought to the space where one is dying—candles, sacred music, scripture, prayer books, communion, anointing or whatever faith symbols to sustain one in trustful dying.

For religious leaders who feel unprepared for this aspect of ministry, a wonderful witness and guide has been provided by Megory Anderson in her book *Sacred Dying*. Out of her ministry with many dying persons and their families, she writes, "No one can truthfully answer the big questions for us, questions like, what is dying like? Will it hurt? What is going to happen to me after I die? Is God going to be there waiting for me? Is God going to be angry at how I lived my life? These questions and fears clearly need to be addressed spiritually and not brushed aside."[21] And then she goes on to describe what she has learned and guides us into spiritually and worshipfully addressing persons in life's final chapter.

To be present to a person and loved ones as death approaches is a hard duty. It is also a sacred privilege! We offer comfort by our presence. We offer simple gifts—scripture reading, prayer, perhaps communion, perhaps anointing—symbols of a greater Grace.

Henri Nouwen spoke of this subject as he remembered his grandmother. He tells of how much she loved him, listening to all his stories of how hard he was working and how much he had to travel. She "was ready to be angry

> Once you accept your own death all of a sudden you are free to live. You no longer care about your reputation . . . you no longer care except so far as your life can be used tactically—to promote a cause you believe in.
>
> —Saul Alinsky

at anyone who could possibly be blamed. Whatever I said, she would always take it so seriously."

As he looked into her face, he saw her eighty years of living, forty-five years of marriage, eleven children, grieving her husband. "Then again I saw her knitting and knitting . . . And sitting in front of me with the rosary in her hands, she said, 'It was so nice that you anointed me that was very beautiful. I think I am ready to go.' And with a smile she added, 'But Henri, you did such a good job I might have to stay a little longer to say more rosaries for the children.' . . . Then—one day, sitting in her chair behind the window, with her old prayer book in her hands, she simply bowed her head and left us. And her face was full of peace and light."[22]

Wouldn't it be lovely to die—and to help others die—as well as she did? We have been exploring steps and conversations that can help us move in that direction.

## THOUGHTS ON HOW TO PROVIDE
## THESE MINISTRIES

We have been exploring education and ministry on death awareness and planning wisely in anticipation of life's end. This is an overwhelming responsibility! Fortunately, this responsibility does not rest on the religious leader alone. There is a growing awareness and a widening variety of helpful resources.

For one thing, there are invaluable print and media resources, free or at a reasonable cost, that are vital aids in guiding people through the steps described in this chapter. "Five Wishes" is available in print or online in various languages at a reasonable cost.[23] The conversation project[24] founded by journalist Ellen Goodman provides helpful free downloadable resources in several languages. In this chapter, I have cited another invaluable resource, also downloadable free, "Caring Conversations." Dr. Angelo Volandes's book *The Conversation: A Revolutionary Plan for End-of-Life Care* and video conversations with him on YouTube offer further insight, accessibility, and wise guidance.

For another, there highly likely are wondrously helpful resource people in your community who can be invited to speak to groups in your ministry and perhaps be further available. Hospice nurses, social workers, or chaplains might be such persons. Geriatricians or Palliative Care specialists could be invited to offer helpful information and perspective.

Older adults themselves, from within your ministry or without, have been on this journey and may well be ready, able, and eager to guide others who want to think about it and make necessary decisions.

There is one step for anyone who would like to be more helpful. That is to do some end-of-life reflection and thinking oneself. This may be done by oneself, with those you love, or with a trusted counselor or guide. There is so much that can be done to make this time of people's lives richer, wiser, and more meaningful. But as in so many areas of ministry, we will not lead persons further than we have gone ourselves.

## FOR REFLECTING AND CONVERSING

1. In your caring ministry, what is the most beautiful death you have experienced/observed? What made it so? The most painful? What made it so?
2. Reflect on the poem "When I am Dying." In what ways does it speak for you? For those with whom you minister? In what ways not? What, if anything, does it leave out?
3. Which might be the most helpful way into leaving behind death denial and entering more fully into death awareness? The *WeCroak* app or one of the conversation books mentioned above? Or?
4. What persons come to mind as resources for end-of-life conversations and activities? Professionals within your congregation? Community persons? One or more of the older adults in your ministry? Or?
5. Where did the chapter remind you of helpful things you are already doing in death awareness and preparation? What invitations did the chapter offer you for further growth in this part of ministry?

## NOTES

1. Kathleen Dowling Singh, *The Grace in Aging: Awaken as You Grow Older*, cited in Lori Erickson, "We Need to Talk About Death," *Christian Century*, August 28, 2019, 21.

2. Matt Fitzgerald, "Shaping My Mind to Die," *Christian Century*, November 7, 2018, 22–27.

3. Vaillant, *Aging Well*, 57.

4. Atul Gawande, *Being Mortal: Medicine and What Matters in the End* (New York: Metropolitan Books, a registered trademark of Henry Holt and Company, LLC, 2014), 55.

5. The Conversation Project accessed November 15, 2019 (www.theconversation project.org).

6. *Caring Conversations: Making Your Healthcare Wishes Known*, published by the Center for Practical Bioethics, accessed November 15, 2019, https://www.practica lbioethics.org/resources/caring-conversations.html.

7. *Caring Conversation*, 4.

8. Richard Coble, *The Chaplain's Presence and Medical Power: Rethinking Loss in the Hospital System* (Lanham: Lexington Books, 2018), 103.

9. Angelo E. Volandes, *The Conversation: A Revolutionary Plan for End-of-Life Care* (Waterville, ME: Thorndike Press, a part of Gale, Cengage Learning, 2015), 49.

10. Gawande, *Being Mortal*, 183–84.

11. *Caring Conversation*, 5–6.

12. Volandes, *The Conversation*, 77–78.

13. Volandes, *The Conversation*, 80–81.

14. Katy Butler, *The Art of Dying Well: A Practical Guide to a Good End of Life* (New York: Scribner, 2019), 90.

15. Butler, *The Art of Dying Well*, 91.

16. Quoted in Butler, *The Art of Dying Well*, 151.

17. Mentioned in Butler, *The Art of Dying Well*, 156.

18. Donna Schaper, *Approaching the End of Life: A Practical and Spiritual Guide* (Lanham: Rowman & Littlefield, 2015), 62–63.

19. Chittister, *The Gift of Years*, 191, 192.

20. Allen Klein, *The Courage to Laugh* (New York: Jeremy P.Tarcher/Putnam, 1998), 71.

21. Megory Anderson, *Sacred Dying: Creating Rituals for Embracing the End of Life* (Boston: Da Capo Press, 2003), 17.

22. Henri Nouwen and Walter J. Gaffney, *Aging: The Fulfillment of Life* (New York: Doubleday, 1974), 61–62.

23. https://fivewishes.org/.

24. https://theconversationproject.org/.

# When I Am Dying

## by Ruth Olson Ralph

When I am dying, make me laugh
Remembering hilarity which crossed our path
(the squeaky fish, the rocking dish,
the jokes we played, the fun we shared)
When I am dying, make me laugh

When I am dying, help me smile
With grandchildren's stories and pictures, and all the while
remembering wonderful times together, and the mile on mile
We travelled to see our loved ones smile.
When I am dying, help me smile

When I am dying, let me grieve
For things undone, for work begun
For hurts imposed unintended and unmended
Because I know there is no reprieve
When I am dying, let me grieve

When I am dying, I must cry
For missed opportunities which passed me by
For children I will never see
Become young men and women grown
It is too hard to say goodbye
When I am dying, I must cry

When I am dying, pray with me
That God will bless my family
And keep them in his loving care.
Then help me go home peacefully
When I am dying, pray with me

When I am dying, hold my hand
Help me know you understand
That I must leave you
And let me go.
When I am dying, hold my hand

(This poem was written by my sister shortly after her husband Roger died several years ago. I think that over the last months of her life, she was able to experience much of what she expressed.)

*Chapter 12*

# Grieve

## *With Us and For Us*

Moses was one hundred twenty years old when he died; his sight was unimpaired, and his vigor had not abated.

—Deuteronomy 34:7

In our death-ignoring and death-denying culture, people may also find it hard to talk about what are their wishes, hopes, and intentions for after their death. Or what will happen to them after they die. Therefore, a valuable gift we religious caregivers can offer older adults is a gentle invitation to discuss these matters. Perhaps we can help them take concrete steps as well as make sure one's wishes are known for when the time of death comes.

### WHAT NEEDS TO BE DONE IMMEDIATELY FOLLOWING A DEATH?

There are some documents and information that should be accessible to one's survivors. This of course would include one's will, any insurance policies, any directions about distribution of intrinsic or extrinsic family treasures, information, keys(!), and access to safety deposit boxes, guidance as to where any currency or other valuables a person may have hidden for a rainy day are. This information should relate anything that needs to be known that one's survivors have access to what material assets and intangible legacy the person left beyond.

Particularly if the person who died is a last survivor, it will be good if religious caregivers know of relatives, friends, and others who should be informed, and who might possibly be involved in making arrangements.

145

Some churches have detailed questionnaires available so that they can be helpful in contacting survivors, if needed. If you are ever in a position where you need to know what to do after a death in greater detail, this website[1] offers that guidance.

## WHAT CHOICES NEED TO BE MADE?

In the days of mourning immediately following a death, there are many decisions to be made. Caregivers can give an advance opportunity for people to plan and notify survivors of these plans and requests.

Over the years, these practices have changed, and so clarity of intention will be helpful. In years past, when someone died, there would be a funeral—usually three days later. And then, usually right after that service, there would be interment and graveside ceremony in a nearby cemetery, perhaps in a family plot. In the months and years after that, family members might visit the grave from time to time, perhaps especially Memorial Day, to care for it, or to remember and perhaps commune with the one who died.

There were some variations in these customs, of course. There might be burial preceding the service, or simply a graveside service. Some might have ritual provided by a lodge or fraternal order. Those who had been in military service might be buried with military honors—with or without other observances. Then as now, there were some who wanted no observance at all. (Further, then as now, some farewell ritual is often more for the survivors, and so, occasionally that "no service" request may need to be overruled.)

In our new, fast-moving, and mobile age, people still die but without the anchors of stable community and place. This is true for elders, but probably it is especially true for their extended families. Intentional planning and discussion are needed to address these topics in a new and different age.

Incidentally, Donna Schaper has found/created a new phrase that I find imaginative and helpful. It used to be when burying the body or spreading the ashes a minister would say "ashes to ashes, dust to dust." Donna now says "star dust to star dust"[2] Whatever one might think of her paraphrase, she notes that it is what people remember and comment about from the service.

## RITUALS, SERVICES, OBSERVANCES,
## NEEDED ACTIONS

Here are some questions to help the elders in your care with their reflection. When you die, what worship-observance-ritual (or none) will be fitting? Do you want the traditional observance of our faith community? Or would you like some variation on that? What music, scripture, other literature do you treasure and would like included in the service? Are there persons you would like to participate?

It is good to write down any requests or wishes about this. When I was a church pastor, from time to time, people would formally or informally tell me some of these things about their wishes. I would make a note and put it into a file folder where such requests went so it would be available when needed.

Now an older adult myself, I have a written reminder to my family about hymns and other music I love, foundational Bible passages, as well as a request for simple modest ways of doing this. They would do this fine, but I do them a favor of not having to figure out these things but follow and adapt my thoughts.

What about the life story/obituary? Often a death notice is put in a newspaper with a brief life story. Further at memorial services, there may be a worship folder that has an obituary. An enriching activity that caregivers can offer is a workshop on writing one's life story in brief compass. (I once experienced a playful introduction to such an exercise—the leader asked us to write out our life story in six words! The one I now recall was "Worked hard but not hard enough.")

Who knows one's life story and who will write it? As for me again as an older adult, I still have a clear memory and know what I would want people to remember. So, I have written mine myself and let family members know where it is. Of course, they will have editorial privileges—I may have said too much or too little. But I have saved them a hard chore when my time comes.

As I earlier mentioned, I have just come back from being with family to celebrate the life and mourn the death of my big sister, Ruth. In the preceding months, knowing that her health and memory were failing, I tried to put together my sister's life story. She had a fascinating life—she was a student at Kent State University and was on campus on the day of the disturbance and shooting. Ruth earned her doctorate there and entered a career of mental health research. She had experienced some mental health issues, hospitalization, and electroconvulsive therapy.

In her work she was a leader in the "Consumer" movement among mental health professionals (those who had received mental health services themselves and provided that perspective). She also did pioneering research and writing in the "recovery" concept of mental health.

Her life story, including her career that ended years ago, should not be forgotten. Since, with her late-life infirmities, she could not write this, I wrote it the best I could. At his request, I had sent this to her son Rob. With modest modifications including family information, that was the life story that the funeral home, church, and local newspaper posted. Friends learned more about her than they had known and were touched by her courageous journey.

## BODY DISPOSAL-USE, DONATION

Further, it is good to help people ask and answer some of these questions— Am I clear about plans for my body? Do my survivors know and concur as to what to do with my body after I die?

A half century ago, only 4 percent were cremated. This has grown to almost 50 percent nationwide; in some states it has increased to almost 75 percent. The Catholic Church eased its restrictions on it in 1963 but still does not encourage it.

Why this change? There now seems to be a variety of beliefs about the role of the physical body/corpse in whatever life there may be on the other side. With families spread, there is less probability of a family plot to visit. There is also flexibility as to when a memorial service can be held and what is to be done with the cremains. These can be buried in one place, divided, or spread over a beloved landscape. This can be done at a flexible time of the survivors' choosing. There are also a wide varieties of ways people have engaged the ashes—embedded in jewelry or paintings, for example.

Cremation is less expensive (average $3,250) than a traditional funeral (average $7,045) with memorial service, less for both if the funeral director is not involved in the funeral or memorial service.[3]

Cremation is also more environmentally friendly than the traditional burial, though not the most environmentally friendly way. There are a small but growing number of "Green Cemeteries" for burial without embalming and in a biodegradable container or none.[4] If anything but the traditional practice of embalming and burial is chosen, this needs to be discussed and decided while people are still living.

## STEWARDSHIP OF ONE'S BODY?

Some years ago, I remember being in a University Student Union, where student nurses were sitting at a booth urging people to sign for donating kidneys or other organs at their death. Playfully one of the nurses would call out to a friend, "Hey Sue, I want your kidneys when you don't need them anymore." It was lighthearted then but also an important reminder. Throughout much of my life, I had the organ donor option stamped on my driver's license.

But when older, pondering of the stewardship of one's body after death changes. With much wear, tear and aging on organs and body tissue, one's organs are likely no longer of use as a donor. For example, I recently called an eye bank to inquire about cornea donation and learned that they do not accept corneas from people over seventy-five years of age. On the other hand, as I browsed the obituary page recently, I read of a sixty-seven-year-old woman who was struck by a car and died. Through the efforts of her physician husband, she "carried out her wish to be an organ donor." The younger of us older adults may have more options than the older among us.

My investigation might be of help to you as you minister with frail older adults. There seemed to be just one place where one's body might possibly be of service after death—to donate it to a medical school for medical education or perhaps research. Recently I went through the process to donate my body to the School of Medicine and Public Health at the University of Wisconsin. In doing so, I learned some things that may be of interest to anyone considering such a step and those who minister with them.

I learned that bodies accepted at that University were solely for medical education and were an important part of that education. Probably my body will be accepted for that purpose, but it is by no means certain. There may be reasons they have to reject it—they do not accept mutilated bodies, ones where an autopsy has been performed, or bodies with various conditions— obesity, malnutrition, hepatitis, jaundice, or some other infectious diseases. (The body can have been embalmed.) When death occurs, their coroner will rule on this, and if accepted make provisions for transporting the body to their facility.

If a body is accepted and used for medical education, it will be cremated at the end of its use (after one or two years) and returned to the family if so requested or else buried with the others on school property.

And so, I do not know for sure if my body can serve this purpose. However—and this is important—it will not even be considered if not pre-registered with the medical school. This is a step that needs decision, conversation with family members, and doing the registration process if it is to happen at all. This practice varies from area to area. So, if one is interested, inquiry and arrangements should be made following the guidelines in one's place of residence.

## CARE FOR THE GRIEVING SURVIVORS

Some time ago, my wife and I had Howard as a houseguest, a man whose wife had died a few months before his visit. The first time I had occasion to greet him, I expressed sympathy and asked him about her sickness and death. He started talking, and continued, going into much detail about her declining health, lengthy hospitalization, and death. He then commented, "This feels so good. Others seemed to be finished with talking about her, but I'm not done yet."

Out of her fresh grief, J. Dana Trent concurs. Two months after her mother's death, she had dinner with a "wise Hindu grandmother." This person asked for specific details about her mother's death. She was "an eager listener—empathically open to hear about Mom's death experience and wanting to know my own perception and reception of it." So comforting was this, that she reflected, "It's a mistaken assumption that the bereaved do not want to recount their loved one's experience."[5]

Too often, we church people are guilty of this omission. We provide lavish care with calls, flowers, meals at the time of death. But then we provide little—or no–support for the difficult months and years afterward. Caring ministry with older adults should include sensitivity about persons' experiences of loss and grief. This and the openness to listen to the grief story again and again.

It is a given that survivors will grieve for a long time after a death or other loss. However, there is infinite variety in what people need and what ministries may be accepted. Veteran pastoral theologian David Switzer has noted the following needs of the grieving person:

1. Identify and express feelings (sadness, hostility, guilt, fear—catharsis).
2. Affirmation of the self.
3. Breaking ties with the deceased.
4. Resurrection of the deceased within the self.
5. Directing one's emotions outward in renewal and deepening of old relationships and establishing of new ones
6. Rediscovery of meaning.[6]

And, out of his rich work in grief counseling and therapy William Worden identifies the tasks of the grieving person.

Task 1: To accept the reality of the loss.
Task 2: To work through to the pain of grief.
Task 3: To adjust to an environment in which the deceased is missing.
Task 4: To emotionally relocate the deceased and move on with life.

Further, he notes, "The culmination will not be to a pre-grief state."[7]

Those are formidable tasks and needs! And if that were not enough, some may have extremely complicated grief. For example, if the person died by suicide, accident, or murder, or if there had been a troubled, conflicted, or abusive relationship, there are emotional scars and wounds that make healing difficult indeed. Sensitive pastoral care, at very least, and quite possibly referral to a mental health counselor with specialties in grief therapy may be needed.

Even apart from troubling complications, each grief journey is unique. J. Dana Trent's reflections are helpful:

> Grief, my therapist once told me, is a unique train ride in which the bereaved are often the sole passengers. It is a long journey through which we remember . . . learn, . . . and receive moments of clarity about who we are without them. There is no fixed schedule . . . and no final destination. . . . There may be some useful anticipated or unanticipated visitors . . . the train may even reverse directions, take an unexpected loop, slow its speed, or accelerate without warning.

Her counselor added, "You are on your train right now, and remember, no two grief trains are alike."[8] She goes on to identify the several distinct stations that came on her unique grief journey.

Dana Trent writes of her grief for her mother while Dana was in her thirties. Is grieving—and ministries of grieving—different for the older population than for people in other life stages?

At very least older adults have experienced enough losses and lived through them, that they do not come to new grieving unaware. They may have developed the emotional "muscles" to live with loss and deal with it. And they may be at peace with what they believe about death and what comes after (a subject we will shortly explore).

At the same time, the experience with deaths of others may be too frequent and too common in the older adult's journey. Loss after loss! Somewhere I heard the quote, "Grief is like DDT—it accumulates." This and other factors will mean there will be wide variation in their preparedness for and response to these times of loss.

Professional religious leaders may offer varied caring actions to minister with the grieving. Grief groups are not for everyone, but for some, such a group can be helpful indeed. An older adult told me of benefiting being a part of such group. In turn, she and another who had the same experience offered the grief group from time to time in their church. For the most part, they found the resource GriefShare useful.[9] The combination of video seminars, support group questions, and personal study was healing and helpful. One participant commented that it was helpful but a little more theologically conservative than she is. Some cherish the chance to speak of their grief and listen to others talk about theirs.

Others may need something different, perhaps quiet one on one listening. They may revisit their loss again and again. For some, a note of remembering the anniversary of the death may be appreciated. As my friend Howard noted, quite likely a person continues grieving long after the rest of the world has gone on.

Another important question for religious caregivers with aging is: What do I do with my own grief in all the loss that comes with loving persons in the last chapter of their lives? It is an honor to be present with people in these times of grief. One needs to be calm, strong, caring. But what can one do to deal with one's own pain of losing loved friends and participants? It is possible to be overcome by grief and loss.

There is an old saying that deaths come in threes, and many a minister has become numbed by grief when several deaths come close together. Whatever heals and renews—time alone, time outside, or enjoyable activities and friendships is essential! This is so one can continue in the important ministry with dying and grieving persons and also be at peace with oneself.

## BELIEFS ABOUT DEATH AND AFTER

The religious caregiver will minister with grieving people who have wide differences in their views of death and what, if anything, comes after. Certainly, it is not necessary to disabuse people of their beliefs. The role of the caregiver is to listen, converse, explore, and, if asked give a report of one's own journey, faith, and reflection on these questions.

### Cultural Influences—Old and New—on Our Beliefs

To begin, become aware how much of what people think about this comes from other sources than the scriptures.

For example, from our humor. A joke starts that someone dies and is first met by whom?—Peter of course. Why Peter? Because—in Matthew 16:13-20, when Jesus asks the disciples who he is, Peter responds, "You are the Messiah/Christ." Jesus blesses his response and said on this, he will build his church, and he will give (Peter? The disciples? The confession?) the "keys of the kingdom of heaven."

One interpretation of this is that God entrusts decisions about who is admitted into heaven to Peter and his successors (through apostolic succession)—the popes of the Roman Catholic Church. But do you believe because of this verse, that "Peter" somehow decides our fate after death? I do not. Do you?

Some views of life beyond this life may have come from classical literature. Many may be influenced, directly or indirectly, by the images from Dante's Inferno, Purgatory and Paradise. The influence may be John Milton's *Paradise Lost* and his portrayal of the penalties of disobedience.

There are also more recent influences. In Charles Dickens's *Christmas Carol*, Jacob Marley's ghost appears from hell and sets Ebenezer Scrooge on a course to discover what he must do to escape hell—and live much more happily in the present!

In another (1946) Christmas classic *It's a Wonderful Life*, the character Clarence Odbody is a soul who has died and is working his way through the ranks of angels. He must help George Bailey see the value of his life in order to get his "Angel-First Class" wings.

The fiction and speculation about the divine, angels, and the hereafter continues in the present. A *Time* magazine article proclaims, "Comedies find surprising new life in the afterlife." In this article, Judy Berman principally describes the TBS comedy series *Miracle Workers* but refers to others including NBC's *The Good Place*, Amazon's *Forever*, and Netflix's *Russian Doll*.

Berman notes that these TV series pose basic questions about human existence. "How do we live good lives? . . .What do we owe to others whether they're strangers or spouses?" The article concludes, "At their best, each one is a challenge to live as though some heavenly arbiter is watching."[10] In so doing, do they add to the cultural folklore about whether there is a life beyond, and if so, what is it like?

The hymns we sing provide images and assurances as well—"In the Sweet Bye and Bye," "I'll Fly Away," and others.

## What the New Testament Says and Does Not Say

As a Christian pastoral theologian, deeply informed by scripture, I turn to the life, death, and resurrection of Jesus and the New Testament to guide me. However, I find the New Testament speaks very little about our life after death. When it does so, it speaks in images, symbols, and metaphors.

Let's look at some of those images and symbols. While dying on the cross, in Luke 23:43, Jesus responded to the repentant criminal also dying, "Today you will be with me in Paradise." Timothy Wengert notes, "'Paradise' here is a Greek word that refers to the enclosed parks of Persian kings, so the paradise pictured here is more of a walk in a beautiful park than as a place 'up there.'"[11]

Another image comes to us from the meditative gospel of John. In John 14:2, Jesus reassures his troubled disciples "In my Father's house there are many . . ." The King James Version had the word "mansions" there. Later translations use the word "rooms," or "dwelling places" or "abiding places." Rather than a specific life after death promise, it is more an assurance of Christ's presence, care, and hospitality to us in this life and the next.

Another New Testament image of the life to come is a banquet. Again, Timothy Wengert notes, "This picture, too, is worth a thousand words because the point is . . . to make it clear being in Christ's presence is sheer joy. For the poor and often hungry people of the first century (and today), no picture expresses joy better than a banquet."[12]

In still another image, the Apostle Paul spoke of threats on his life. And then, he stated the core of the hope that sustained him, "to depart and be with Christ, that is far better." (Philippians 1:23b). What is the life after this life, Paul? It is to "be with Christ."

Donna Schaper counsels us, her fellow ministers, "Don't be afraid of metaphors. Sometimes they are all we have."[13] And sometimes, these images pry open talk about what one believes, trusts, finds helpful, and doesn't find helpful.

## The Alternative—Hell

What about the other possibility—separation, or "hell"? In the Old Testament, there seems to be a shadow place of dwelling after death, "Sheol" in Hebrew, "Hades" in Greek, and sometimes translated "hell" in our scriptures (e.g., Psalm 139:8 in the King James Version). In Matthew 5:24, Jesus urges acts of piety and integrity so as not to be liable to "hell"— Gehenna in the Greek, a burning garbage pit outside of Jerusalem. In some of Jesus's parables, people can choose to live out God's love and be rewarded or not do so and be punished (for example, Matthew 25:31-46). In the book of Revelation, there are more vivid descriptions of the punishment of the wicked. Here again, we contemporaries seem to say more about it than our Bible does.

## Conclusion

And so, as we bring our questions about what is after death to the New Testament, we are given images and metaphors. It's like a walk in a garden, a lavish banquet, a room—an abiding place—in God's hospitality. It is to be "with Christ" which is to be treasured beyond this life.

While the New Testament provides little description, it offers strong affirmation. The New Testament makes clear that Jesus's death and resurrection was not just about him, but about us as well. In John 11: 25-26, Jesus boldly promises, "I am the resurrection and the life. Those who believe in me, though they die, will live, and everyone who lives and believes in me will never die."

---

Eleanor Roosevelt on the afterlife, "Whatever it is, I daresay I shall be able to cope with it."

---

That's a promise, a few hints, a few clues, much less than popular culture has filled in over the centuries. Krister

Stendahl, Lutheran Bible scholar, theologian, and bishop, wisely counseled, "Say neither too much nor too little concerning what lies beyond death. Not too much, because we speak of what we cannot know. But not too little, for while we cannot comprehend who we will be, we know something trustworthy of who God is."[14]

## And Yet

And yet, I am not quite finished with what informs and guides my belief about life beyond. Something that points in this direction is the reported experiences of people who have been near death or who have been clinically dead, and somehow have come back. In particular, I am invited into the mystery by what a dear friend, Dave Johnson, humbly and quietly told me. In his early thirties just when he was well into his career as a social worker in his state's corrections system, Dave suffered an extremely severe heart attack. For days he hovered between life and death.

One day, laying in his bed in his hospital room, he became aware of bright light coming through a window that had billowing white curtains. He felt his being gently drawn in his bed toward the light. (Probably, no one else would have seen the light or the curtains or the moving bed.) After a time, gradually he felt the bed moving away from the window and the light dimming. He understood the light to be death and beyond. And though he enjoyed his career and dearly loved his wife and young children, he felt disappointed at not being able to go to the light.

His firsthand account to me is in harmony with other near death or clinical death restorations about which I have read. Being drawn to the light, to a place of great peace—that is the testimony of those who have been close. Those experiences guide and invite me.

## AND SO

Though there is little description the New Testament gives as to what life after death is like, there also is the assurance throughout the New Testament that a rich new life with God in some form awaits us. This takes us back to Matt Fitzgerald's story started in the previous chapter.

As mentioned earlier, Matt had found the app *WeCroak* with its five time a day reminder "Don't forget you're going to die" helpful to him. It aided in calming him and giving him perspective and humility.

In time, Matt became aware of the conflict between the philosophy behind the app and his Christian faith. He wrote "*WeCroak* thinks death is natural. Christianity says death is obscene. Worse than that, *WeCroak* can make you happy. The risen Christ can give you joy. So delete the app!"

He concludes, "I won't forget. I'm going to die. For now, I'm trying to remember something else. We will rise again. I turned *WeCroak* off."[15]

As for me, I believe that what I experience of God's graciousness and love here and now—the family love, the friendships, the joy, the laughter, the beauty, the ecstasy—are foretaste what my relationship with God will be on the other side.

In my forty years of being a pastor, I conducted hundreds of funerals, most of them for brothers and sisters in my faith, partners in the life and witness of the church to which we both belonged. Almost all of those funerals ended in the same way—I would share the scripture affirmation I claim for them and for myself. That is the stirring promise in Romans. "For I am convinced that neither death, nor life . . . nor anything else in all creation will be able to separate us from the love of God in Christ Jesus our Lord" (Romans 8:38-39).

## FOR YOUR REFLECTING AND CONVERSING

1. What are your wisest and most effective strategies for supporting grieving persons? What gaps and omissions do you sense in that care? What more do you feel led to attempt, to offer?
2. How do you deal with your own grief as you offer care in a population where death is more frequent?
3. What is your experience and feeling about the changed practices when death comes—cremation and so on?
4. How would you describe your journey and beliefs as regards death and what is after? What have been your experiences in ministering with people asking these questions?

## NOTES

1. "Your To-do List after a Loved One Dies," accessed April 4, 2020, https://www.verywellhealth.com/survivors-checklist-after-death-1132601.

2. Schaper, *Approaching the End of Life*, 8.

3. "Cremation in America," accessed November 20, 2019, http://www.slate.com/articles/business/moneybox/2015/05/cremation_rates_in_the_u_s_a_state_by_state_map.html.

4. "Green Burial Sites in the United States," accessed March 31, 2020, http://www.us-funerals.com/funeral-articles/directory-of-green-burial-sites-in-the-united-states.html#.XoNgbXdFyUk.

5. J. Dana Trent, *Dessert First: Preparing for Death While Savoring Life* (St. Louis: Chalice Press, 2019), 19.

6. David K. Switzer, *Pastoral Care Emergencies* (Minneapolis: Fortress Press, 2000).

7. J. William Worden, *Grief Counseling and Grief Therapy: A Handbook for the Mental Health Practitioner* (New York: Springer Pub. 1991, 2002).

8. Trent, *Dessert First*, 60–61.

9. "How GriefShare Works," accessed March 31, 2020, https://www.griefshare .org/about.

10. Judy Berman, "Comedies Find Surprising New Life in the Afterlife," *Time*, February 18–25, 2019, 106.

11. Timothy J. Wengert, "By the Light of Grace: How Does the ELCA Understand Heaven and Hell?" *Living Lutheran* 3, no. 7 (October 2018): 15.

12. Wengert, "By the Light of Grace," 16.

13. Schaper, *Approaching the end of Life*, 78.

14. Quoted in Wengert, "By the Light of Grace," 18.

15. Fitzgerald, "Shaping My Mind to Die," 27.

*Chapter 13*

# Getting There

Young men and women alike, old and young together!
Let them praise the name of the LORD.

—Psalm 148:12

How does a caring community develop a creative, deeper, and wider-ranging ministry with older adults? I will share four vignettes of churches who are doing this, each in their own way. These stories may stir creativity and offer possibilities. And then we will reflect on what this says to each of us in our unique settings.

## LAKEVIEW LUTHERAN CHURCH, MADISON, WISCONSIN—A COMMUNITY-MINDED CHURCH

When I called and asked to talk with the minister, the secretary responded, "He's here, but he can't come to the phone. He is baking biscuits." This was my introduction to a unique ministry.

This northside Madison church has about 800 people on its role, a worship attendance of 100–150. It has a long history. Lakeview began as an outpost of St. John's Lutheran in downtown Madison. The congregation organized in the early 1800s. The first structure was built in 1884 and is still periodically used on grounds today. It is near the huge Oscar Maier meat processing and packaging plant that was bought out and closed down a few years ago. There are two state institutions nearby, one for persons with mental disabilities, one for people with mental illness. These three industries are where most of the people in the congregation and neighborhood work or have worked. Pastor Dean Kirst

159

summarizes, "We are middle or lower middle class. We are not a wealthy congregation, not prestigious or colorful. There are no doctors, professors, or state officials in our membership. We are mostly a blue-collar congregation in a blue-collar neighborhood, and as a result, we don't live beyond our means."

In 2010, when the associate pastor left, the congregation explored what would enrich the life of their congregation and its outreach. They discerned they wanted more adult Bible studies, senior social activities, and some emphases in worship. It was learned from the congregation that they did not want services specifically designated as "traditional" or "contemporary" but that a mix of music and styles should be incorporated into every worship service that is offered. And so, they hired a part-time ministry coordinator who has helped to make these things possible. Out of these decisions, preceded by the church's longtime openness to surrounding community, and Pastor Dean Kirst's playful relational style, ministries with older adults have developed and expanded.

For example, they have a monthly senior lunch and euchre tournament. Eighty or more persons from church and neighborhood take part. Pastor Dean, a cooking enthusiast, takes the leadership on these meals, recruiting older adults to help prepare, for example, peel potatoes, and do cleanup. The meal is geared to senior needs. Pastor Kirst grew up in central Wisconsin and knows what foods they probably had as children. Each summer, they had a couple of grilled meat meals since many seniors cannot do that anymore. They have served Irish stew, rice pudding, soul food, cow heart, chicken gizzards. "I had people come just to have chicken gizzards."

There are also fun day trips and longer senior trips that have grown into needing a thirty-two-seat bus. All these trips are geared to senior interests, needs, and ambulation, including wheelchairs. Care is given to be sure that all activities are accessible to any who would like to go.

There have also been frequent intergenerational mission trips—traveling to Biloxi, MS, New Orleans, LA, Minot, ND, and Crisfield, MD. Dean recalls, "In these many trips, we did lots of hard work and met wonderful people in horrible situations. People come back from those experiences changed and with a special bond with each other."

This church has identified and claimed older adult leadership in numerous ways. For example, a retired baker has offered baking classes, eagerly attended. Another older adult chairs the food pantry available every Monday afternoon and evening, and she is ably assisted by many other seniors. Older adults chaired and accomplished fund-raising campaigns for a renovated kitchen and air-conditioned social hall.

Spiritual growth is stimulated through worship and both Sunday morning and weekday Bible studies. As to worship, "We are very not formal. If you want to come in shorts and a t-shirt, come ahead."

Pastor Dean has also discerned that his officiating at many funerals for members and nonmembers alike has offered spiritual hope as faith encounters the end of life. He notes, "Funerals are a place where people want me there and I feel I really have purpose—the relationship of the gospel to human lives. The person who died has shared the gospel in some way in their life, and I try to talk about that."

Several years ago, the church tackled the issue of covenanted bonds between people for whom a state-licensed wedding was not possible or preferred. They considered offering an opportunity to make a "household covenant" including, if wanted, a service of blessing at the church. Persons desiring this might include older adult couples, those who cannot choose legal marriage because disability funding or other public financial sources would be affected, as well as gay, lesbian, bi-sexual, or trans-gendered couples.

Dean recalls, "I learned that when you take an issue like that, some of the most supportive and open-minded people are 80 years old or older." It was within the senior community in this congregation where the most support came to look beyond tradition, orthodoxy, and ritual.[1]

When I asked if any older adults had benefited from this new policy, Dean replied, "Yes, a senior couple did take advantage of the household covenant. I conducted a service for them in the chapel at Waunakee Manor Nursing Home. I did exactly what we do for a wedding service. The only thing missing was a state purchased marriage license. They did this because of senior benefits and beneficiaries. All their children and grandchildren were present, and it was a great celebration. We had the service there so that the bride's 90 something old mother could attend."

While many people assume that seniors will stand in the way of change, that was not Pastor Dean's experience with the community at Lakeview. Congregations often fear they are becoming older. This pastor would encourage those congregations to build on the strength of a senior population. Open the doors to seniors from the community. Always consider the way that that senior population can enhance and provide intergenerational activities. These can happen not only on the premises but in other locations, away from bricks and mortar.

## ORCHARD RIDGE UNITED CHURCH OF CHRIST, MADISON, WI—INTENTIONALLY INCLUSIVE

As I open the web page of this congregation, I read—

"Spiritually Alive, Joyfully Inclusive, Committed to Justice . . . Orchard Ridge UCC is a member of the United Church of Christ. We consist of approximately 500 members from the Madison/Dane County area. We are a progressive congregation trying to make the Christian faith relevant in today's world. We are deeply committed to social action, a vibrant worship life, and a ministry with children and youth. We welcome visitors and guests at all our functions. . . . We welcome theological inquiry, insights from other faiths, and those with serious questions and doubts. Seekers and doubters abound in our midst among guests and members alike."

They go on to identify as "an Open and Affirming church, a Sanctuary Church, and a church that value[s] children." There is also this word on the first page "Wheelchair accessible, hearing-assist devices, and large print bulletins available."[2]

Though the web page has no other specific reference to older adults, this is a church that has implemented a vital and many dimensioned intergenerational community life.

It may be as basic as attention to language. For example, they became aware that the title they gave to their church retreats, "Church Family Retreats" was unintentionally exclusive. They changed the name to "All Church Retreats" and made an effort to include all ages. This worked and has led to much more intergenerational sharing.

It also involves pastors' inclusive attitudes and efforts. When I asked one of the ministers, Tammy Martens if she sees playfulness among older adults, she answered, "All the time. They tease me, and I tease them. That is just part of my way of being in the world. Even when things get serious, we somehow find ways to laugh. Elders are the ones who can see humor and hope in a serious situation." Further, each ministry staff meeting devotes attention to what pastoral needs older adults might have and who among the staff is responding to those needs.

A much-enjoyed activity has been when the fourth and fifth grade class creates a game to play with older adults and then invites the older adults to play it with them. The fourth and fifth graders spend eight weeks in pairs creating and designing a Board Game that they will play with elders on a Sunday morning during Sunday School. Pastor Tammy who created and guides this activity notes, "The kids LOVE creating their own Board Game. Once they have their Board Games finished, we select a Sunday morning date for them to play the game with some elders. Each 4th/5th grade pair is matched up with two or three elders. They use conversation cards throughout the game, which helps them get to know each other better." This activity is repeated every two years, with the succeeding group of fourth and fifth graders. This relational activity has now been experienced three times, and it has increased friendship and two-way storytelling between the generations.

This has led to many friendships. For example, one older man, Steve, has learned the names of the children and youth in the church. "He readily connects with youth. He is fun hearted, knows the young people all by name, and is a great storyteller—a true bridge builder. When he has a choice where to sit at a church meal, he sometimes sits with the young people talking with them and hearing their stories," Tammy reports.

Another place where older adults interact with youth is as chaperones on the youth mission trips. Persons in their sixties or seventies enjoy being a part of this weeklong trip with teenagers, working side by side with them on work projects. There have been these joint youth and supporting adult outreaches to Alamosa, Colorado, working with Habitat for Humanity, Greensboro, North Carolina helping build tiny houses for veterans, and Birmingham Alabama, painting houses for low-income families and learning about civil rights.

She reflects, "There has to be thoughtfulness about what you can do to make this happen. It's not that we are doing this all that well, but we do have people thinking about the intergenerational piece and frequently acting on it."

A woman who is in her seventies, Sara, is deeply involved in addressing climate change, lobbying, and journeys to DC to witness to this agenda. Another, Jan, organizes a women's book club that meets at the church once a month. She is a lifelong learner, open to new ideas, joyful and with a command of the English language. Still another older adult, Steve, recently drove a load of supplies to the Texas-Mexico border to aid in refugee ministries there. And another has made several trips to the border. All of these people are in their seventies. Last fall, seeing the need for clothes among these refugees, the church asked the youth if they would be interested in organizing the clothes drive. The youth loved doing this and they were beautifully, supported by caring adults.

There are also many older adults involved in the choirs, handbells, and other music offerings of the church.

One aspect of their ministry that works beautifully is "pastoral partners." A person in the congregation partners with someone who may be infirmed, widowed, housebound, or simply in need of a caring friend. The pastoral partner is in touch with their assigned person at least once a month. And every other month, the pastoral partners meet with minister Ken Jennings for reflection and further skill development. At the time of this writing, there were nineteen pastoral partner relationships. Older adults are on both ends of this program—both caregivers and care receivers.

What sorts of things do these pastoral partners do? It takes many forms. For example, driving them to an appointment or bringing them to a program at church, visiting them in the nursing home, cooking a meal for or with them, playing a game with them, taking them to a movie, and more. Some of the pastoral partners are diligent in keeping the ministers informed of special needs or crises in their care receivers' lives.

A place where older adults explicitly minister with older adults is the "Over 55" meal and program that meets once a month. There is an older adult who plans the programs, enlists the speakers, and conducts the sessions. Those who gather are fed lavishly by the "catering mission team." Historically, the meal was organized as a potluck. It was noticed, however, that there wasn't much variety and sometimes not enough food was brought. This was solved about five or six years ago when some people, who joined the church and had a passion for cooking, decided to plan and cook the meal for this group. Their largest overall task is the monthly Over 55 gathering, but they also are called upon for other church events—picnics, memorial service meals, and celebrations. Those who attend Over 55 are asked to make a donation, just for the cost of the food—a modest contribution for an excellent meal, enjoyed at round tables of fellowship. Around sixty to eighty people attend this monthly gathering.

The pastors see much room for growth of these ministries. They wish they knew more ways to engage the gifts of other elders. For example, there is a family with an older man who has difficulty hearing and getting around. Still, his family says he is bored and wishes he had something to do. How to engage the gifts of such a person remains a challenge.

Further, pastors sometimes wish older adults would be more transparent about problems, crises, and needs. Later they might say to a pastor, "Oh, I just didn't want to bother you." The older people may want their privacy, want to tough it out, or don't want to bother other people. One minister opines, "Perhaps this is a Midwest attitude, maybe a Midwest German attitude."

On the other hand, they experience many older adults where being part of a church helps give meaning to some of their finer legacies and helps them see they are connected with the generations. They are led to understand this is a place where they can make a contribution to the generations beyond them. The church is a place where people can act on their passions. Pastors help them launch something they could not otherwise do by themselves.

## BLUE VALLEY KANSAS CHRISTIAN
## CHURCH—A DEVELOPING PARADIGM

Blue Valley Christian Church (BVCC) was in a time of transition. They were looking for somewhere to worship and also a place to serve. They found both in the same location!

In 2014 the congregation, which once had been much larger, had shrunk to the point they no longer needed, nor could they afford, maintaining their large building. So, they sold their building, and for a couple of years, "embedded" at another church of their denomination. (That is to say, they rented space so that they could carry on their worship and other activities but did not seek to merge with that church.) As their narrative describes it, "We . . . discerned that God was not finished with us. So rather than become a legacy church [close and donate all the resources from their sale to some other ministry or cause], we became a remnant church, earnestly seeking God's will and purpose." With income from the building sale, they were not "strapped for cash," and so they had some time to study and explore.

This remnant congregation of some twenty-five members investigated several possibilities of ways they could be missional and helpful. Eventually, they discovered the right fit. As their narrative tells it, "We were led to Silvercrest at Deer Creek where our eyes have been opened to the need for this kind of ministry."[3]

Silvercrest at Deer Creek is a for-profit retirement community, a part of the Dial Senior Living Communities. It has approximately 112 residents and 65 staff members, and it provides two levels of care, independent and assisted living. The assisted living includes both those with dementia and those who do not have dementia but need an extra level of care.

And so BVCC investigated worshipping within and offering ministries to this retirement community. Pastor Lois Kelley describes the arrangement between church and retirement community—"It's very informal. We do not have anything in writing, just a verbal agreement. We have a place to worship and don't pay rent, and they get a free chaplain and a congregation of volunteers."

For three going on four years, a little congregation and a retirement community have been developing a common life together. A small number of community residents, up to fifteen, worship when the church gathers on Sunday, perhaps more for special occasions such as the annual memorial service. The worship is "older adult friendly" with spaces for walkers and wheelchairs, no expectations of standing during the service, and Lord's Supper, where participants may choose to come forward for the elements or be served where they sit.

Beyond worship, the congregation engages with the retirement community in a wide variety of ways. They provide holiday celebrations, storytelling workshops, and other activities. They invite residents into joint ministry projects, such as aiding a public-school teacher to provide read at home books for her students and writing to these students.

As many residents had or have pets, another favorite outreach activity is to provide bean bag heating pads for the KC Pet Project. The residents help make the bean bags which can be heated in the microwave and used for injured animals or animals recovering from surgery.

They also have a book group with shared leadership. This group meets twice a month and discusses a chapter or two of the selected book. These discussions often lead to elders sharing their stories and wisdom.

Pastor Lois devotes three days a week as a volunteer chaplain to the community. This might be spent in visiting people's apartments, counseling times,

> As Desmond Tutu told me on a recent trip to Cape Town, "We are only lightbulbs, Richard, and our job is just to remain screwed in."
>
> —Richard Rohr,
> *Falling Upward*

or being visible and available in the community gathering places. Or she might be in the "Serenity Room" a space within the library with devotional materials, and she can be of help to persons seeking aids for their spiritual journey.

She also offers twice a week activities with people in assisted living that are much appreciated by both residents and staff. Lois relates, "Many times we play trivia type games, such as life stories, farm questions, etc. This usually triggers conversations about their growing up years." Sometimes, she has located pictures of a resident's hometown and brought these to the group, which often stirs forgotten recollections. She then gives the pictures to the resident from that town.

BVCC offers a vital alternative to the occasional worship service some congregation might provide but not be seen again for months on end. Rather, they have been a constant, caring presence. Trust and respect have grown. Pastor Lois reflects, "If residents have a need, a confusion, a loss, a hurt, or spiritual questions they come to us." Her ministry is extended to both staff and residents.

She has also sensed something of a division between the independent living and the assisted living portions of the community and so she is helping to bridge that division. Some of this arises from residents' fears of leaving independent living. Pastor Lois discerns that for some, this fear is bigger than the fear they faced with leaving their home and going to independent living.

The church simultaneously reaches out inclusively and maintains a distinct identity. Here is part of their self-description: "BVCC is a community that defines itself as a mission connection center where people gather for encouragement, spiritual growth, knowledge and opportunities to apply their gifts, experiences, and interests toward living out the ongoing ministry established by the Christ."

BVCC does not see this ministry as an end in itself. Rather they believe they have found another paradigm for ministry in these changing times. They want to make their experience known and invite others into similar ministries. A first step in this is their creation of a Senior Adult Chaplaincy Internship Program. They will recruit a fairly compensated chaplain intern to work with them for a six-month term (which can be renewed for one more term).

Their recruitment document says in part,

Chief among the many insights gleaned from BVCC's accidental journey into a senior adult chaplaincy is that individuals 65+ living in independent and assisted living communities represent America's most rapidly growing vulnerable and underserved populations. We believe our journey has useful implications for future or displaced ministers seeking an alternative rewarding career path. This internship is . . . opportunity to both learn about potentially robust and critically needed ministry, and to gain real-world experience in a congregation pioneering senior adult chaplaincy as a new way to be church.

They also make their website and Facebook page available and anticipate offering workshops to invite others into their newly discovered and much-loved ministry. A brochure they created announces. "A Church Reimagined: wilderness journey leads to pioneering a new mission and vision of ministry." They have indeed found new life offering ministry with older people and invite others to join in this important new trend.

## IMMANUEL BAPTIST CHURCH, BROOKFIELD, WISCONSIN A MISSIONAL CHURCH TO, WITH, FROM OLDER ADULTS

On their website, Immanuel Baptist Church introduces itself with these words—"We are committed to multiplying disciples and creating missional communities throughout the greater Milwaukee area and empowering others to do the same in their local communities." Among the core values that guide them, "We believe that the kingdom of God is emerging all around us and that Jesus Christ is calling us to seek and follow him where He is among the broken and marginalized of our communities."[4]

In order to be a voting member of this church, one is asked to do four things: worship regularly, give in a scheduled way, participate in some spiritual growth group, and engage in a missional outreach. Older adults are not exempt from this!

Their commitment to being missional has led them into engagements on a number of fronts. For our purposes, we will focus on their outreach among older adults, particularly the vulnerable among them.

I asked their pastor, Max Ramsey what changes he has seen among older adults in the last twenty years. He responded, "Seniors are more and more housing insecure and food insecure. People find themselves trapped in food deserts. Changing demographics have created insecurities. Crime rates are going up in those neighborhoods."

I next asked Max what problems or hardships he experienced in his ministries with the elder poor. He responded, "For me, it's secondary trauma, the moral wound of being unable to help people. Health support for mental health issues is just gone. It's so hard to have people reach out for assistance and there be no assistance for them to turn to. Retirement income is inadequate for many. For some, there is a sense of social isolation that is devastating. The lack of transportation adds to their sense of isolation."

"Another area of difficulty is home care support. I know of a man who fell and needed home care, and no one could help him until a social worker—6 weeks to 3 months later—could do an evaluation. In such times, there will probably be a visit the emergency room of a hospital—at 10 times the cost."

Aware that one church cannot address these massive needs alone, for twenty years, Rev. Ramsey has been searching for and locating agencies that are they are what they say they are. He then has found ways to network with those groups and agencies to work together with them.

One of Immanuel Church's response has been a food pantry, "Despensa de la Pax" (pantry of peace) in partnership with Friedens Community Ministries. This is located in one of the most underserved neighborhoods on the Southside of Milwaukee.

They have chosen not to accept federal funding and the restrictions that go with that. They do receive help from Feeding America, and so they are able to serve people from any zip code and to give help more than once a month if needed. Their website notes that in the previous year "Despensa de la Pax was able to provide 3-5 days of healthy food to 26,000 individuals."

Every Saturday morning, there is organized chaos as leaders, volunteers, and people with food needs converge on their pantry site. Some needing food come without identification. Those who regularly receive help are asked to come every other week. But nobody is turned away.

Sarah, a volunteer who checks people in tells me, "I would not want to help in a pantry that has to turn hungry people away. I couldn't do that." When registering, the person tells the number of persons in their household, and this determines the quantity of food they can select. All are treated with kindness and respect, an expression of God's grace that has brought them together. When a box of donuts broke open, a volunteer offered them to all close by. When a child spilled a drink and looked worried, another volunteer quietly mopped it up.

Older adults are among those who receive food and also among the volunteers who provide the services needed to make this work. Mary, in her seventies, is one of the volunteers who makes this place "tick." I asked Mary about the journey that brought her here. She responded, "I've been in several churches. The Pentecostals taught me how to worship and pray. Then I met Pastor Max and he added depth. I respect him as his daily life is a teaching in depth. There is a song 'Humble, Kind,' That's what I see in him, and that is what I want us to be."

I asked her what it was like volunteering each week. She answered, "There is a mixture of ages here. We work together well. We've nothing to prove—we are all volunteers. We are family without strings." When I asked her what her volunteer role was, "I organize and clean—stuff and people. I am always cleaning, putting things away." And she was called away from our conversation to do just that.

She is one of many volunteers. As I talked with others, I learned they came from many different churches and from no church. Max notes that 600 to 700 people regularly serve in this or one of the other ministries, and many of them are not part of their worshipping congregation.

In the same section of Milwaukee, they participate in a ministry called StreetLife Communities. When I asked Max what that ministry offered, he responded that they offer the same things out on the street that they do in the pantry—caring, perhaps help with food or clothing, support, and care. Older adults are among the street people served. Max reflected, "There are people on the streets, who are eligible for AARP (which starts at the age of fifty). Some in their 60s, but life is harsh. Many do not live very far into their 60s."

A couple of times every three months, Immanuel folk provide a meal for the community kitchen at Saint Benjamin the Moor Church in downtown Milwaukee. Their website encourages this as "opportunity to provide a hot meal to people with few resources." This opportunity is offered as "a fantastic opportunity to invite friends who don't know the Lord to come and see."

What about faith development and spiritual life among the older adults in this ministry? Rev. Ramsey reflects and responds, "This is more generational. Young people tend to be sprinters—not going to something every week for a long time. Older folks are marathoners. They will come every week to talk for a while, share prayer concerns, Bible studies, and spiritual support. For some groups that is enough, but one group is different. They are an inter-generational group. The oldest member is 100. They have a quick report on prayer concerns and then get to work making the meals for our homeless and St. Ben's ministries."

Playfulness and laughter abound in these groups and activities. "Anything that happens anywhere else. They don't get old inside, just get old on the outside."

What about older adults finding meaning and purpose in their present life? Max responds, "I'm a little bit existential on that. We don't find meaning—we make meaning. It matters because it has to matter. Take that meal making group. They made their own meaning. They made that ministry. They show up because it is important for them to show up. And now I am at a point if that group ceases to be, I couldn't replace it."

In the ministries of Immanuel Church, older adults share their passion and leave a legacy. As Max observes, "They know they are planting trees they will never sit in the shade." He notes that he hears no complaints about younger people. Rather they are open to listen and counsel with those in struggles along their life journey.

Max concludes, "I don't want to be part of a community without seniors in it. They get it. We are like parents. Open the building. Be there for them. Seniors are like grandparents. They send cards and remember others. I want babies and hundred-year-olds in a community I serve."

## WHAT DO WE LEARN FROM THESE CONGREGATIONS AND THEIR MINISTRIES?

Where did I find, and why did I choose to describe these four churches and ministries? Two of them were suggested to me by colleagues. For the other two, I was intrigued by an interview with one of their pastors and asked permission to explore them further. I worshiped at two of these churches, visited a ministry of another, and had no contact but correspondence with the other. (That pastor was a former seminary student of mine.)

I started investigating each of these because they sounded positive and enthusiastic about older adults. At the beginning, I was intrigued but had no preconceived notion what I would learn from them. And so, at this point, I ask myself as well as you, what do we learn from these stories? These churches are from four different denominations, different sizes, different settings, and with a fair amount of theological diversity among them. What do they have to tell us?

A starting place, though sometimes unstated, is an appreciation and openness to older adults. While I did not inquire about timetables, it appeared that increased involvement with seniors developed slowly. There were various attempts to engage, marked by reflection and evaluation, leading to further engagement. Trust must be built, and trust has to be earned by reliable caring over the months and the years. Each of them found at least one thing they did very well and built upon that.

As to specifics, there are a few items that are mentioned more than once among these churches. At least two had hospitable and delicious meal events that the adults greatly enjoyed. Two of them participated in food pantries where older adults were both among the workers making it possible as well as among those who received the help. At least two mentioned adventurous travel, both for missional serving and for enjoyment.

If I understand these pastors correctly, they came to their effectiveness in a basic way. They built on their strengths, or they sensed a new need among older adults and tried to respond in a caring way. Their ministries evolved and grew out of what they had already put in place.

I also sensed something of surprise among these pastors when I wanted to tell of their church. They did not feel they were doing anything unusual. They were just being attentive to ministry with all ages and generations, separately and in conversation with each other.

## HOW DO WE MOVE INTO MORE EFFECTIVE MINISTRY AMONG OLDER ADULTS?

As with the churches I described, your growing edge may be beginning with some aspect of ministry that you are already doing well and considering whether this could be offered to a wider community.

Or it may begin with intentional study and conversation. That is how it happened with one church. Shepherd of the Bay Lutheran Church in Ellison Bay, Wisconsin lived with the awareness that they were an aging church in a county that had the highest median age of any county in the state. Their pastor, James Honig called the church to join in a study of a large and extensive book, *Elderhood: Redefining Aging, Transforming Medicine, Reimagining Life.* by Louise Aaronson.[5] This book, written by a gifted and respected geriatrician, raised many issues that people were hearing for the first time. It had an impact on Pastor Honig as well. He reflected, "Most of my ministry, I have not seen old people in the rich mosaic that Aaronson sees in her book. A first gift is to see older adults both in their unique needs, and in the gifts that they may have to enrich local congregation and the wider world."

Their study prompted the church to create a task force to investigate and, by the end of the year, to launch a ministry of health and wellness, primarily for older adults. It is already clear that one of the components of this ministry will be to employ a parish nurse. There will be more to come in this focused congregation.

If a congregation does not respond to book discussion experiences, perhaps a film night or series could raise interest and begin the conversation about ministry possibilities. In appendix B, there is a list of movies that may say something interesting about aging. This might be aging itself, or end of life, or dementia, or other fascinating perspectives on older adults.

A step into new possibilities might come from intentionally doing focused interviews with a number of older adults, both in your congregation and in the wider community you serve. In his book, *An Age of Opportunity: Intentional Ministry By, With, and For Older Adults,*[6] Richard Gentzler provides much guidance on how to discern ministry direction through surveys as well as intentional interviewing and listening to older adults.

He provides many tools for discovering the greatest needs to which a ministry can respond. Gentzler's publisher has graciously granted me permission to include one of his older adult interview designs. You will find it in appendix A. I particularly appreciate the page where there is listed a number of items that might be part of older adult ministry. With each of these, there are two questions—Do you need? and Can you provide? In this way, he is opening the door to the possibility that some of the ministries that older adults need can be provided, at least in part, by older adults themselves.

## AND SO

For me, researching and writing this book has been a lovely adventure. I started from my own ministry journey and aging journey and went on to interviews, observations, discussions, field trips, and living in a retirement community. My goal was to learn more about my contemporaries and what best ministry with them looks like. I have also met so many fabulous and gifted authors in my library studies.

I have told you what I discovered, and now I am about finished. How I hope that good things will come out of this, that ministers, churches, and older adults will see each other in a new light, a new mission opportunity revealed. In language that I engaged earlier, I have been passionate about this project. If it stimulates interest and effective ministries, I will count it among my legacies.

As I draw this chapter to a close, I hope I did not over promise with my chapter title, "Getting There." Only you know the how of doing that in your setting. I have told you the best that I know. The next chapters will be written by you.

## FOR REFLECTING AND CONVERSING

1. How are you feeling about your ministry with older adults? What do you celebrate? Where do you mourn? Where do you long? Where do you wonder?
2. What church or pastor did you most identify with? Where is the story of your ministry similar? Different? What ideas or suggestions did you take from those stories?
3. What class, board, group, or organization (or the whole church) might be open to a book study, such as the Ellison Bay Lutheran Church did? What book might be helpful in introducing a vaster older adult ministry?
4. What is one thing you will commit to do to extend your ministry with elders just a little?

## NOTES

1. "Lakeview Lutheran Policy on Household Covenants," accessed April 2, 2020, lakeviewlutheranchurch.org/wp-content/uploads/2014/12/pol-affirmationdocume nt.pd.

2. "Orchard Ridge United Church of Christ," accessed April 2, 2020, https://www .orucc.org/.

3. "Blue Valley Christian Church – About Us," accessed April 2, 2020, https://ww w.bvcc-silvercrest.org/about-us.

4. "Immanuel Baptist Church," accessed January 23, 2020, https://immanuel-church-brookfield.com/.

5. . Aronson, *Elderhood*. See also James Honig, "Review of *Elderhood: Redefining Aging, Transforming Medicine, Reimagining Life* by Louise Aronson," *Christian Century*, December 18, 2019.

6. Gentzler, *An Age of Opportunity*.

# Postscript

## *Ministry with Older Adults after the Pandemic*

Indeed, he is going ahead of you into Galilee. There you will see him.

—Matthew 28:7b

What if we can choose to experience this liminal space and time,
this uncomfortable now, as . . . a place and state of creativity,
of construction and deconstruction, choice and transformation?

—Sheryl Fullerton[1]

As I have noted earlier, this book was proposed and mostly written before the pandemic occurred. It was refined and submitted during the pandemic. As it begins the process of being prepared for publication some of the social isolation and stay at home orders are being softened. There are cautious steps in allowing some businesses to reopen with safety guidelines in place. And churches are pondering how to make transitions back at least some physically present events.

I believe that most of what I wrote pre-pandemic is still valid and applicable. Still, there is much speculation about what the church will be in post-pandemic times. The more pressing question for our purposes is this: Within this changed church, what will ministry with older adults be like in the aftermath of these strange and difficult times?

This response, in turn, has at least two aspects. For one, what *will* be possible—what is reasonably safe with testing and possible new vaccines? For the other, what *should* this ministry be—what have we learned to help pastors and churches be more sensitive, responsive, and redemptive? What have seniors learned about their faith, churchmanship, justice concerns, and vital Christian practices?

As to the first question—what is possible—it appears that many activities that once were greatly enjoyed will not be possible for quite some time. For example, Pastor Dean Kirst notes that at least temporarily, the monthly meal and euchre tournament—ninety or more adults together in a confined area, enjoying each other, the food, and the competition, won't be possible. Nor will the short- and long-term bus trips, with thirty or more in close proximity for hours or days on end happen, at least not for quite a while. As mentioned in chapter 13, these were aspects of the vigorous ministry with older adults at Lakeview Lutheran Church.

Crowded sanctuaries, joyous hymn fests, choir festivals, holding hands in a friendship circle, delicious banquets and potlucks, reassuring hugs, commonly shared Bibles and hymnbooks—all this must change and be given up, at least for a time. If or when these are again possible, something may have shifted in our consciousness. Our view of church and gatherings may have lost or changed some of these expectations.

But what may we gain and learn from all this? What *should* ministry with older adults look like?

## GROWING WHILE ALONE

For one thing, I hope that persons of all ages learn from the isolation—how to do time alone and quietness more effectively. Earlier I mentioned Joan Chittister's observation that "Aloneness is the new monastery of the elderly."[2] The pandemic caused persons of all ages to live confined to their homes, their "new monastery." Of course, some of those monasteries were crowded, with perhaps two parents working from their residence, making room for young adults back from university, and home schooling their children. Still there are lessons to be learned from the slowing down and withdrawing all were required to do. Darrel Lackey writes, "We are all monastics now." And there is opportunity to engage this perspective in the slowing down. Perhaps we can prepare ourselves for whatever is next. He points out, for example, that when monks withdraw from the world, still they are present to the world in creation, in prayer, in communion, in embracing the world. Our scriptures also give us the example of John the Baptist who came out of a time of preparation in the wilderness.[3] Perhaps we can learn how to turn our loneliness into solitude and discover how to pray and how to care about our world and the direction of our nation in a new way.[4]

This mutual experience of isolation experiences with older adults can lead in another fruitful way. It can make people aware of how much loneliness hurts. It can stir awareness of ways to include elderly persons who are alone—include them for meals, for conversation, for holidays.

## REFLECTION AND ORAL HISTORY

This leads to another possibility. It comes from the awareness that we have lived through a unique historical event. Many more people died than died in the 9/11 attack. There are more deaths than from the Vietnam and Korean war episodes combined.

Further, people have had to be isolated from loved ones in nursing homes, care facilities, and hospitals during frightening times. All of us have been deeply touched in some ways during this pandemic. These times call for reflection, discovery, and storytelling. There comes a time to ask what have we learned from all this?

Older adults may have something unique to offer in such times of reflection. We olders may have a little longer view and perspective. For example, if someone asked me, "Have you ever been through something like this before?" I would respond, "Not exactly, but in some ways, yes."

I might tell of the winter, when I was serving my first little rural church, just out of seminary. Blizzards came five or six weekends in a row so that no one among my all farmer congregation could come to church. Then for weeks after, country roads were first so snowy and then so muddy. When I tried to call on these families, I got stuck time and again. Finally, they asked me not to call on them until the snowy-muddy season passed. No seminary class had prepared me for being minister when my efforts to care were more trouble than they were worth! It was an earlier time when I was asked to help by staying out of the way and preparing for fruitful caring in whatever way I could. This was a small preview to experiencing stay at home orders.

Or I might tell of the fright when the polio epidemic (called infantile paralysis back then) increased precipitously. Water activities seem to exacerbate it, and swimming pools, water events, and festivals were closed. One teenager in our youth fellowship caught it, leaving his legs impaired and his view of life very downcast.

I might also tell about the excitement when the Salk vaccine was developed. I remember the exciting community events, as people by the hundreds, registered, walked by a table, picked up a sugar cube with the vaccine in it and swallowed it.

Others might recall the tragic times when so many were infected and dying of AIDS until, finally, medications and treatments developed. I was not as directly affected by that, but I did lose a good friend and former parishioner to that dread disease.

I am suggesting that religious leaders and communities see their elders as repositories of wisdom and memory. This may lead to more sensitive and patient listening. Or it could evolve into living history projects to capture memories and insights for individuals and communities, including churches.

The memory and wisdom may go beyond quarantines and pandemics to other perspectives, valuable for relearning how to be the church today.

## INCREASED USE OF TECHNOLOGY

There is another trend that will continue after the worst of the confinement is over, and that is increased use of technology. Many possible technologies are available. Some of these may respond to various needs for a community of people who cannot gather as freely as they once did. Some technological platforms make possible one way oral and visual communication. Others provide opportunity for group participation.

All of these require some equipment and the knowledge of how to engage them. For some elders, probably mostly the older of us, this is no small barrier. I was touched by Ruth Everhart's description of trying to teach her mother the community program "Zoom" and, of course, doing it remotely. She and her mother often used the simpler, one on one "Facetime" program to visit, but Ruth hoped for a whole family gathering on Zoom for Easter. She writes of her mother "She was born into the Great Depression and is tougher than she looks. She soldiers through my instructions about 'icons' and 'apps' and 'links' bravely using words she does not comprehend. She does understand that when she touches certain configurations, things open on her tablet like magic. Until they don't . . . . Then I tell her to press the home button and we try again." She adds, "The hours we spend struggling to establish this new connection feel as sacred as any I have ever spent on Good Friday."[5]

For those who have found their way through the technology maze, there are some pleasant surprises. I recently heard a pastor describe her church's experience. At the beginning, they had little previous experience. And so, they underwent a steep learning curve as to how to make worship available to those isolated in their homes.

But gradually, they discovered good things starting to happen. Persons who had left that church but not connected to a new one started listening in. Inactive members and others in the community tuned in. Rather than engaging fewer persons, they were engaging more. She concludes that when social distancing ends, they will still offer some form of worship ministry for those who cannot/do not come to the church building. This lovely surprise and responding strategy is shared by many other pastors and churches.

With continuing practice, groups gathering remotely can discover how to be present and helpful to each other. For example, Wayne DeHart tells of being a part of a small group that had been meeting face to face. When the social distancing orders came, they continued to meet using the Zoom technology. As the group met on Zoom recently, he noticed that one of the participants was much more quiet than usual. He followed up with a phone call, learned that the person was struggling with depression, and could offer support over the phone.[6]

With a little coaching, isolated older people can feel at least a little less isolated through the various platforms of modern technology.

## CHANGED USE AND CHANGING BUILDINGS

The post-pandemic church will also have some decisions to make about their buildings. Barry Howard writes of discoveries during the pandemic. One he mentions is "A campus [building or buildings] is a valuable resource of the church, but it's not a church" He continues, that a building "can be an important tool for a congregation, but it is just one of many tools in a congregation's toolbox."[7]

Indeed, church buildings may need a second look. Many congregations have long had a larger building than they needed. The future church may need even less space. And the space should be safe and accessible to older adults and other persons with special needs. At very least, these qualities are needed: well lighted, bright, welcoming, friendly, warm, wide doors and hallways, handrails, minimum of stairs, accessible bathrooms and kitchens that can accommodate a wheel chair or walker.

Perhaps old buildings will need to be sold or repurposed. A fruitful discussion may be, how can our building be a tool for our mission here and beyond? What is no longer needed? Recall the story of Blue Valley Christian Church in chapter 13—they are doing vital ministry with no building at all.

## SUPPORT FOR THE STRESSES AND STRAINS

Another thing where consciousness may have been raised during the stay at home times—it got boring and irritating. This was true both for care givers and for care receivers. In our residential community, for a while the changes were made and followed with good cheer. Residents learned to isolate, except for walks outside with masks on. Staff developed strategies to deliver groceries, meals, pharmaceuticals, and whatever else was needed to our doors. These services were received with gratitude and praise.

But it grew old—for everybody. Delays and mistakes became more irritating. The temptation for residents to just get in their cars, go out, and do the shopping for themselves grew stronger. Some who were single grew lonelier. Some who were married got on each other's nerves. And yet, much of this was exactly what the frailest among older people live with every day of their lives!

There were learning opportunities in those moments. For one, there is the need to be sensitive to mental health issues for all elders, but especially isolated ones. Chronic pain, loneliness, depression, anxiety can happen.

Max Ramsey noted all the troubling conditions surrounding all of us but particularly isolated older people. There are health concerns about COVID-19 as well as worsening economic issues with so many out of work. There is political unrest, polarization, and stagnation. And there are all too frequent times of racial tension over a killing or unjust decision. He is not at all surprised that some of the older adults in his ministry seem to be gripped by a generalized or perhaps chronic anxiety.[8]

The retirement community where Lois Kelley offers ministry sensed more and more signs of strain among their residents. And so, they worked with Lois to give all those living there a flyer telling them that she was available for a Zoom or FaceTime chat. They did not call it grief counseling, or crisis intervention, just a chat—about whatever they wanted to talk about.

This was a good start, but even more might be needed. Older people live with all the issues younger ones do—depression, anxiety, bipolar issues, substance abuse, and more. Further, the longer one lives, the more vulnerable that person is to the various dementia and memory issues. At the same time, mental health agencies are developing the way to offer counseling and therapy remotely. Religious leaders can serve will by being aware both of signs that elders need more help and of the agencies that can offer support.

Another learning from those strained times is how much each person—including the old and especially the isolated old need a quiet word or act of kindness, and they need it often. As Arthur Caliandro, wisely advised, "Be kinder than you think it is necessary to be because the other person needs it more than you know."[9]

## RECOGNITION OF RESILIENCE AND RESOURCEFULNESS OF ELDERS

The pandemic also showed us that older adults are more resilient and more creative than others might imagine. We have already mentioned how many tackled the unfamiliar tasks of engaging the new media platforms. But their resourcefulness went beyond that. Many older persons sewed masks, not only for themselves but for their families, fellow residents, staff persons, and those in hard hit areas.

Further, in the retirement community where I am, an appeal went out for the desperate need of the agency that supplies many food pantries in our community. And the elder residents responded with gifts totaling well over $12,000 to feed the hungry.

Properly distanced, we provided humor, music, and entertainment to each other. The responsible persons found a way to write, publish and circulate our monthly newspaper and to fill it with news of the good and caring things people are doing here. The paper also welcomed the new persons who have made their way to their new home here in these strange times. We have helped each other thrive, even as was widely known, older people were among the most vulnerable to COVID-19 infection.

A frequent theme in this book has been the opportunity to claim the giftedness of many older adults to enrich the life of their faith communities. Responses during the pandemic underline and undergird that assertion!

## GROWING CONCERNS AND SHRINKING INFLUENCE

I find among other older adults what I sense within myself—a growing concern about many things in our nation and world paired with despair at how little energy, activity, or influence I have about these matters.

For example, global warming. As I think about our world, I am convinced of the wisdom of the "Seven Generation" teaching of the Iroquois nation. It guides us to think seven generations ahead for the impact of the actions we take today. Seven generations comes to 140 years or more.[10]

Last summer my first two great grandchildren were born—the fourth generation from me. I am thinking forty years ahead and hope so deeply that when these bright little boys are adults, they live in a safe world. I hope that their world is not a dangerous one, past the tipping point of global temperatures, filled with even more violent storms and dangerous weather than is happening now. May we all act now to avoid that and to create a brighter future.

Another concern is about support and care of the elderly who are not as fortunate as I am. In chapter 2, there was discussion about where ageism, and sexism, or racism, or both came together. The impact is almost always poverty and less access to needed services. The fate of these fragile populations is rarely mentioned, not even in the campaign rhetoric of politicians, much less what they do.

Another concern is the deterioration of relationships between the various races and the ethnic groups in our nation. The celebrated victories of past years seem to be reversed and the antagonism and violence even worse.

And another is the polarization and paralysis of the government to govern!

With all this, I and my fellow elders are older with less energy, mobility, resources to make much impact on this troubling picture. And so, a hope for the post-pandemic ministry with older adults is that such passions are addressed. Older adults may be limited, but there are gifts we can give, conversations we can have, letters we can write, and organizations to whom we can give resources. Even if we cannot do much, we can be a part of something great. I hope for leadership on that from the post-pandemic church.

## A SHARP AWARENESS OF
## VULNERABILITY AND MORTALITY

The pandemic does raise one other ministry need. As Ron Mach put it, "Older adults like me are rethinking our confidence in the actuarial tables that give us years to live. A C-Virus among us can sharpen mortality awareness. Ministers and lay leaders new a new awareness that mortality is not an Ash Wednesday liturgical event but a daily fact of life for young but especially older adults."[11]

In chapters 11 and 12 we spoke of helpful conversations to prepare for end of life issues and how to honor those who die and support those who grieve. It was also acknowledged that many avoid these things out of death denial and ignoring death. A crisis like this may create a new openness to talk with family, religious leaders, and medical providers about wisely addressing the end of life.

## AND SO

While there is much we do not know, some of the broad outline of ministry with elders after the pandemic is becoming clearer.

As Wayne Shannon, the chaplain of Oakwood Village—Prairie Ridge where I live, well summarized. "I only know that I will do the ministry to which I've been called. A ministry of listening, walking with, and allowing seniors to share their stories in the midst of life changes. That will not change, but how we go about it might . . . . We share, we serve, we witness . . . in whatever form that might take now or after the pandemic."[12]

## FOR REFLECTING AND CONVERSING

1. What did you miss most during the stay at home orders? What did you miss most about your ministries with older adults?
2. What fresh and unexpected opportunities for ministry, if any, did you experience during the stay at home and social distancing time?
3. Who are some of the people you most admire for what they did during the pandemic? Are there older adults among them? If so, who, and why?

4. In what ways are you refocusing and reimagining your ministry with older adults out of these changed times?
5. How has this historical time impacted your theological convictions? Your ministry and mission strategy? Your understanding of how and what the church is, at its best?

## NOTES

1. Sheryl Fullerton, "'What Else is There,' 'Liminal Space,'" *Oneing* 8, no. 1 (2020): 77–78.

2. Chittister, *The Gift of Years*, 144.

3. Matthew 3:1-6.

4. Darrel Lackey, "We All Monastics Now," May 9, 2020, https://www.patheos.com/blogs/divergence/2020/05/09/we-are-all-monastics-now/https://www.patheos.com/blogs/divergence/2020/05/09/we-are-all-monastics-now/.

5. Ruth Everhart, "What Language Can I Borrow?" *Christian Century*, May 6, 2020, 12.

6. Wayne DeHart, email correspondence, May 26, 2020.

7. Barry Howard, "7 Things Your Church Can Learn During This Global Pandemic," *Ethics Daily*, April 27, 2020, https://ethicsdaily.com/7-things-your-church-can-learn-during-this-global-pandemic/.

8. Max Ramsey, phone conversation, June 2, 2020.

9. As quoted in Mitch Carnell, "COVID-19 Makes It Crucial to Be More Thoughtful with Your Words," accessed May 29, 2020, https://ethicsdaily.com/covid-19-makes-it-crucial-to-be-more-thoughtful-with-your-words/.

10. "Seven Generation Sustainability," accessed June 3, 2020, https://en.wikipedia.org/wiki/Seven_generation_sustainability.

11. Ron Mach, Email correspondence, April 26, 2020.

12. Wayne Shannon, Email correspondence, April 26, 2020.

# Appendix A

## *Sample—Older Adult Survey*

Name:_____

Address:_____

_____

Phone #:_____Email Address:_____

Gender: Female  Male

Date of Birth:_____

Marital Status: Married    Single    Never Married    Divorced   Widowed

Do you live alone? Yes No

If no, with whom do you live? _____

In the event of an emergency, if you need help or became ill or disabled, is there someone to whom you could turn for assistance? Yes No

If yes, who? _____ Relationship: _____

Address:_____ Telephone #_____

During the past week, how many times did you:

  Have someone visit you? _____ Visit someone else? _____

  Go shopping? _____ Talk with a friend or relative on the telephone? _____

Do you experience any problems with where you live? Yes No

If yes, what are the problems? _____

Please rate your health: Excellent    Very Good    Good    Fair    Poor

Approximately how often do you attend religious services?

  Weekly    Twice a month    Monthly    Quarterly    Yearly    Never

Would you like to receive any of the following religious services in your home?

  Pastoral Visitation    Lay Visitation    Devotional materials    Bible study materials    Holy Communion,    Other:_____

185

| Do You Need? | | | Can You Provide? | |
|---|---|---|---|---|
| Yes | No | Transportation | Yes | No |
| Yes | No | Home Repairs | Yes | No |
| Yes | No | Housekeeping Chores | Yes | No |
| Yes | No | Minor Plumbing Repairs | Yes | No |
| Yes | No | Minor Carpentry Repairs | Yes | No |
| Yes | No | Legal Counsel | Yes | No |
| Yes | No | Income Tax Preparation | Yes | No |
| Yes | No | Financial Counsel | Yes | No |
| Yes | No | Medical Assistance | Yes | No |
| Yes | No | Meal Preparation | Yes | No |
| Yes | No | Reading Materials | Yes | No |
| Yes | No | Support Group | Yes | No |
| Yes | No | Fellowship Group | Yes | No |
| Yes | No | Bible Study Group | Yes | No |
| Yes | No | Prayer Group | Yes | No |
| Yes | No | Caregivers Support Group | Yes | No |
| Yes | No | Respite Support | Yes | No |
| Yes | No | Travel Opportunities | Yes | No |

Other Need(s) You Have: _____

_____

Other Ministry You Can Provide: _____

_____

Please identify or list any programs the church (or seniors' group) should provide for older adults: _____

_____

Name of Interviewer:_____ Date: _____

"Sample Older Adult Survey" is taken from the book *An Age of Opportunity: Intentional Ministry by, with, and for Older Adults* pages 199–202 by Richard H. Gentzler, Jr. Copyright Ⓒ 2018 by Richard H. Gentzler, Jr. and published by Discipleship Resources, Nashville, Tennessee. All rights reserved. Used by permission.

# Appendix B

## *Movies of Interest*

### ABOUT OLDER ADULTS

*Alive Inside.* 2014

Filmmaker Michael Rossato-Bennett's documentary chronicles the astonishing experiences of individuals with dementia around the country who have been revitalized and awakened by the simple act of listening to the music of their youth.

*The Farewell.* 2019

After learning that her family's beloved matriarch, Nai Nai, has been given mere weeks to live, Chinese-born, U.S.-raised Billi returns to Changchun. Billi is forever changed by her grandmother's wondrous spirit.

*On Golden Pond*, 1982

In a lovely classic film, an older couple makes peace with their daughter.

*Tuesdays with Morrie*, 1999

Journalist Mitch Albom reunites with and learns from his college mentor.

*Away from Her*, 2006

A touching drama of the effects of Alzheimer's disease on the patient and on others.

*Still Alice*, 2015

Alice Howland is a renowned linguistics professor who starts to forget words. When she receives a diagnosis of Early-Onset Alzheimer's Disease, Alice and her family find their bonds thoroughly tested.

*Iris*, 2001

When Iris Murdoch begins experiencing forgetfulness and dementia, the ever doltish but devoted John struggles with hopelessness and frustration to become her caretaker, as his wife's mind deteriorates from the ravages of Alzheimer's disease.

*The Intern*, 2015

The plot follows a seventy-year-old widower who becomes a senior intern at an online fashion website.

*The Best Exotic Marigold Hotel*, 2011

British retirees travel to India to take up residence in what they believe is a newly restored hotel. Less luxurious than advertised, the Marigold Hotel nevertheless slowly begins to charm in unexpected ways.

*The Bucket List*, 2007

Two terminally ill men escape from a cancer ward and head off on a road trip with a wish list of to-dos before they die.

*Philomena*, 2013

A world-weary political journalist picks up the story of a woman's search for her son, who was taken away from her decades ago after she became pregnant and was forced to live in a convent.

You might find other movies about older adults of interest. This website offers some other possibilities: https://www.imdb.com/list/ls059549875/

# Bibliography

Adler, Hilde. *I Am Not Old Enough! The Twenty-Seven Stages of Adjustment to Living in a Retirement Community.* Amherst, MA: Modern Memoirs Inc., 2019.

"Aging and Life Course." Accessed March 13, 2020. https://www.who.int/ageing/ageism/en/.

Anderson, Megory. *Sacred Dying: Creating Rituals for Embracing the End of Life.* Boston: Da Capo Press, 2003.

Applewhite, Ashton. *This Chair Rocks: A Manifesto Against Ageism.* Networked Books, 2016.

Aronson, Louise. *A History of the Present Illness.* New York: Bloomsbury, 2013.

Aronson, Louise. *Elderhood: Redefining Aging, Transforming Medicine, Reimagining Life.* New York: Bloomsbury Publishing, 2019.

Backman, Maurice. "The Frightening Reason Many Americans Retire Earlier Than They Planned." Accessed December 31, 2019. https://www.msn.com/en-us/money/retirement/the-frightening-reason-many-americans-retire-earlier-than-planned/ar-BBYungY?ocid=spartanntp.

Baker, Beth. *Old Age in a New Age: The Promise of Transformative Nursing Homes.* Nashville: Vanderbilt University Press, 2007.

Bankson, Marjory Zoet. *Creative Aging: Rethinking Retirement and Non-Retirement in a Changing World.* Nashville: Skylight Paths, 2010.

Bass, Dorothy (ed.). *Practicing Our Faith*, 2nd ed. San Francisco: Jossey-Bass, 1997, 2010.

Bauer, George. *The Seasoned Traveler: A Guide for Baby Boomers and Beyond.* Guilford, CT: Insiders' Guide, an Imprint of the Globe Pequot Press, 2006.

Benson, Herbert and Eileen Stuart (eds.). *The Wellness Book; The Comprehensive Guide to Maintaining Health and Treating Stress-Related Illnesses.* New York: Birch Lane Press, 1992.

Berger, Peter L. *Redeeming Laughter: The Comic Dimension of Human Experience.* New York: Walter De Gruyter, 1997.

Bergstrom, Richard and Leona Bergstrom. *Third Calling: What Are You Doing the Rest of Our Life?* Edmonds, WA: Re-Ignite, a division of ChurchHealth, 2016.

Berman, Judy. "Comedies Find Surprising New Life in the Afterlife." *Time*, February 18–25, 2019.

Bianchi, Eugene. *Aging as a Spiritual Journey*. Chestnut Ridge, NY: Crossroad, 1984.

Bimstock, Robert H. "In Memoriam: Bernice L. Neugarten." *The Gerontologist* 42, no. 2 (2020): 149–51.

Blezard, Robert C. "By the Light of Grace: How Does the ELCA Understand Heaven and Hell?" *Living Lutheran*, October 2018.

Brokaw, Tom. *The Greatest Generation*. New York: Random House, 1998.

Brokaw, Tom. *Boom! Voices of the Sixties: Personal Reflections on the '60s and Today*. New York: Random House, 2007.

Brokaw, Tom. *A Lucky Life Interrupted*. New York: Random House, 2015.

Buchanan, Missy. *Living with Purpose in a Worn-Out Body*. Nashville: Upper Room Books, 2016.

Buffet, Bill. "#026260 A Prisoner's Story, Continued." *Baptist Peacemaker*, July–September 2018.

Butler, Katy. *The Art of Dying Well: A Practical Guide to a Good End of Life*. New York: Scribner, 2019.

Butler, Robert N. *Why Survive? Being Old in America*. Baltimore: The Johns Hopkins University Press, 1975.

*Caring Conversations: Making Your Healthcare Wishes Known*. Kansas City: Center for Practical Bioethics, 1999, 2013.

*Caring Conversations: Making Your Healthcare Wishes Known*, published by the Center for Practical Bioethics. Accessed November 15, 2019. https://www.practicalbioethics.org/resources/caring-conversations.html.

"Changes in Life Expectancy in the United States." Accessed January 4, 2019. https://www.seniorliving.org/history/1900-2000-changes-life-expectancy-united-states/.

Chittister, Joan. *The Gift of Years: Growing Older Gracefully*. New York: Bluebridge, 2008.

Coble, Richard. *The Chaplain's Presence and Medical Power: Rethinking Loss in the Hospital System*. Lanham: Lexington Books, 2018.

Collins, Sonya. "Is 100 the New 80? What's It Take to Live Longer?" Accessed January 7, 2019. https://www.webmd.com/healthy-aging/news/20180920/is-100-the-new-80-whats-it-take-to-live-longer.

"Cremation in America." Accessed December 1, 2019. http://www.slate.com/articles/business/moneybox/2015/05/cremation_rates_in_the_u_s_a_state_by_state_map.html.

Damask, Kevin. *Columbus Journal*, "Ex-Teacher's Property to be Auctioned Sat." Reported in *Wisconsin State Journal*, October 23, 2019.

Doheny, Kathleen. "6 Ways Your Body Gets Better with Age." Accessed March 12, 2020. https://www.everydayhealth.com/senior-health/ways-your-body-gets-better-with-age/.

Dychtwald, Ken. *Age Power: How the 21st Century Will Be Ruled by the New Old*. New York: Jeremy P. Tarcher/Putnam, 1999.

Dychtwald, Ken and Daniel J. Kadler. *With Purpose: Going from Success to Significance in Work and Life.* New York: Collins Living, an Imprint of Collins Publishers, 2009.

Emmons, Robert A. *Thanks! How the New Science of Gratitude Can Make You Happier.* Boston: Houghton Mifflin Company, 2007.

Erickson, Lori. "We Need to Talk about Death." *Christian Century,* August 28, 2019.

Erikson, Erik. *Childhood and Society.* New York: W.W. Norton and Company, 1950.

Esar, Evan (ed.). *20,000 Quips & Quotes: A Treasury of Witty Remarks, Comic Proverbs, Wisecracks, and Epigrams.* New York: Barnes & Noble Books, 1968.

Fitzgerald, Matt. "Shaping My Mind to Die." *The Christian Century,* November 7, 2018.

Foster, Richard. *Celebration of Discipline.* San Francisco: HarperSanFrancisco, 1978, 1998.

Fowler, James W. *Stages of Faith.* New York: Harper and Row, 1981.

Frankl, Viktor E. *Man's Search for Meaning: An Introduction to Logotherapy.* New York: Washington Square Press, 1963.

Frankl, Viktor E. *The Doctor and the Soul: From Psychotherapy to Logotherapy.* New York: Vintage Books, 1986.

Gawande, Atul. *Being Mortal: Medicine and What Matters in the End.* New York: Metropolitan Books, a registered trademark of Henry Holt and Company, LLC, 2014.

Gentzler, Richard H., Jr. *An Age of Opportunity: Intentional Ministry By, With, and For Older Adults.* Nashville: Discipleship Resources, 2018.

"Green Burial Sites in the United States." Accessed March 31, 2020. http://www.us-funerals.com/funeral-articles/directory-of-green-burial-sites-in-the-united-states.html#.XoNgbXdFyUk.

"Healthy People – Older Adults." Accessed March 12, 2020. https://www.healthypeople.gov/2020/topics-objectives/topic/older-adult.

Holden, Wendy. *Born Survivors: Three Young Mothers and Their Extraordinary Story of Courage, Defiance, and Hope.* New York: Harper Perennial, 2015.

Honig, James. "Review of *Elderhood: Redefining Aging, Transforming Medicine, Reimagining Life* by Louise Aronson." *Christian Century,* December 18, 2019.

Jenkinson, Stephen. *Come of Age: The Case for Elderhood in Time of Trouble.* Berkeley: North Atlantic Books, 2018.

Kahn, Andrew. "Cremation in America." Moneybox Commentary about Business and Finance. Accessed February 5, 2019. http://www.slate.com/articles/business/moneybox/2015/05/cremation_rates_in_the_u_s_a_state_by_state_map.html.

Kimble, Melvin A. (ed.). *Viktor Frankl's Contribution to Spirituality and Aging.* New York: The Haworth Pastoral Press, 2000. Simultaneously published as *Journal of Religious Gerontology,* Volume 11, Numbers 3/4, 2000.

Kleiber, Shannon Henry. "The Power of Music and Memory: 'Music Was Waking Up Something Within Each of Them.'" Accessed January 6, 2020. https://www.ttbook.org/interview/power-music-and-memory-music-was-waking-something-within-each-them.

Klein, Allen. *The Courage to Laugh.* New York: Jeremy P. Tarcher/Putnam, 1998.

Koch, Tom. *Mirrored Lives: Aging Children and Elderly Parents.* Westport, CT: Praeger, 1990.

Koenig, Harold and Andrew Weaver. *Counseling Troubled Older Adults: A Handbook for Pastors and Religious Caregivers.* Nashville: Abingdon, 1997.

Koenig, Harold and Andrew Weaver. *Pastoral Care of Older Adults.* Minneapolis: Fortress, 1998.

Laslett, Peter. *A Fresh Map of Life: The Emergence of the Third Age.* Cambridge: Harvard University Press, 1991.

Loe, Meika. *Aging Our Way: Lessons for Living from 85 and Beyond.* New York: Oxford, 2011.

MacKinlay, Elizabeth. *Spiritual Growth and Care in the Fourth Age of Life.* London and Philadelphia: Jessica Kingsley Publishers, 2006.

MacKinlay, Elizabeth, James Ellor and Stephen Pickard (eds.). *Aging, Spirituality, and Pastoral Care: A Multi-National Perspective.* New York: Haworth Pastoral Press, 2001.

"Maggie Kuhn Quotes." Accessed August 24, 2019. https://www.thoughtco.com/maggie-kuhn-quotes-3525374.

Martenson, Roland B. *Elders Rising: The Promise and Peril of Aging.* Minneapolis: Fortress Press, 2018.

Martz, Sandra Haldeman (ed.). *Grow Old Along with Me the Best Is Yet to Be.* Watsonville, CA: Papier-Mache Press, 1996.

Masko, Meganne K. "Music Therapy and Spiritual Care in End-of-Life: A Qualitative Inquiry into Ethics and Training Issues Identified by Chaplains and Music Therapists." *Journal of Music Therapy* 53, no. 4 (2016): 309–35.

Mayo Clinic. "Stroke." Accessed March 14, 2020. https://www.mayoclinic.org/diseases-conditions/stroke/symptoms-causes/syc-20350113.

Mayo Clinic. "Parkinson's Disease." Accessed March 14, 2020. https://www.mayoclinic.org/diseases-conditions/parkinsons-disease/symptoms-causes/syc-20376055.

McCullough, Charles. *Head of Heaven, Feet of Clay.* Cleveland: The Pilgrim Press, 1981.

Menzies, Laurie L. *Embracing Elderhood: Planning for the Next Stage of Life.* Buffalo: Embracing Elderhood Press, 2014.

Moore, Thomas. *Ageless Soul: The Lifelong Journey Toward Meaning and Joy.* New York: St. Martin's Press, 2017.

"Music for Life: The Story of New Horizons." Accessed March 23, 2020. https://www.wxxi.org/musicforlife.

National Institute on Aging. "Hearing Loss: A Common Problem for Older Adults." Accessed March 14, 2020. https://www.nia.nih.gov/health/hearing-loss-common-problem-older-adult.

Nouwen, Henri and Walter J. Gaffney. *Aging: The Fulfillment of Life.* New York: Doubleday, 1974.

Nusbaum, Martha C. and Saul Levmore. *Aging Thoughtfully: Conversations about Retirement, Romance, Wrinkles and Regret.* New York: Oxford, 2017.

O'Donnell, Liz. *Working Daughter: A Guide to Caring for Your Aging Parents While Making a Living.* Lanham: Rowman & Littlefield, 2019.

Olson, Richard, Ruth Lofgren Rosell, Nathan S. Marsh, and Angela Barker Jackson. *A Guide to Ministry Self-Care: Negotiating Today's Challenges with Resilience and Grace.* Lanham: Rowman and Littlefield, 2018.

Palmer, Parker. *On the Brink of Everything: Grace, Gravity, and Getting Old.* Oakland: Berrett-Kohler, 2018.

Pipher, Mary. *Another Country: Negotiating the Emotional Terrain of Our Elders.* New York: Riverhead Books, 1999.

Pipher, Mary. *Women Rowing North: Navigating Life's Currents and Flourishing as We Age.* New York: Bloomsbury Publishing, 2018.

"Poll: 1 in 4 Have no Plans to Retire." Associated Press, found in *Wisconsin State Journal* 7/8/2019.

Ramsey, Janet L. "Holy Friendship: Reimaging Ministry with Homebound Older Adults." *Word & World* 26, no. 3 (Summer 2006): 259–68.

Rohr, Richard. *Falling Upward: A Spirituality for the Two Halves of Life.* San Francisco: Jossey-Bass, 2011.

Schade, Leah. "Hi, I'm Leah. I'm a Recovering Racist." Accessed August 24, 2019. https://www.patheos.com/blogs/ecopreacher/2019/01/recovering-racist/?u tm_source=Newsletter&utm_medium=email&utm_campaign=Progressive+Ch ristian&utm_content=43.

Schaper, Donna. *Approaching the End of Life: A Practical and Spiritual Guide.* Lanham: Rowman & Littlefield, 2015.

Scheib, Karen. *Challenging Invisibility: Practices of Care with Older Women.* St. Louis: Chalice, 2004.

Schneider, David. *Arrows of Light: Devotions for Worldwide Christians.* Kearney, NE: Morris Publishing, 2005.

Shapiro, Evan. "A Humble Solution to Global Depression." *Time*, February 18–25, 2019.

Sherman, Edmund. *Contemplative Aging: A Way of Being in Later Life.* Los Angeles: Gordian Knot Book, an imprint of Richard Altschuler & Associates, Inc., 2010.

Singh, Kathleen Dowling. *The Grace in Aging: Awaken as You Grow Older.* Somerville, MA: Wisdom Publications, 2014.

Smith, Brian. *Closing Comments: ALS–A Spiritual Journey into the Heart of a Fatal Affliction.* Jacksonville Beach, FL: Clements Publishing, 2000.

Starita, Joe. *The Dull Knifes of Pine Ridge.* 2nd ed. Lincoln, NE: Bison Books, 2002.

Stevens, R. Paul. *Aging Matters: Finding Your Calling for the Rest of Your Life.* Grand Rapids: William B. Eerdman's, 2016.

Stobbe, Mike. "US Life Expectancy Dips." AP, found in *Wisconsin State Journal* November 23, 2018.

Sullender, R. Scott. *Losses in Later Life: A Way of Walking with God.* New York: Haworth Pastoral Press, 1999.

"Supporting Older Patients with Chronic Conditions." Accessed March 12, 2020. https://www.nia.nih.gov/health/supporting-older-patients-chronic-conditions.

Swinton, John. *Dementia: Living in the Memories of God.* Grand Rapids: Eerdmans, 2012.

Switzer, David K. *Pastoral Care Emergencies.* Minneapolis: Fortress Press, 2000.

"The Challenges of our Aging Society." Accessed November 15, 2019. http://www .aging.wisc.edu.

The Conversation Project. Accessed November 15, 2019. https://www.theconversa tionproject.org/.

"The Global Network for Age-friendly Cities and Communities: Looking Back Over the Last Decade, Looking Forward to the Next." Accessed March 23, 2020. https:/ /extranet.who.int/agefriendlyworld/.

Tornstam, Lars. "Gerotranscendence in a Broad Cross-Sectional Perspective." *Journal of Aging and Identity* 2, no. 1 (1977).

Trent, J. Dana. *Dessert First: Preparing for Death while Savoring Life.* St. Louis: Chalice Press, 2019.

Trevitt, Corine. "Chapter 8 Meeting the Challenge: Older People with Memory Loss and Dementia." In Elizabeth MacKinlay, *Spiritual Growth and Care in the Fourth Age of Life.* London: Jessica Kingsley Publishers, 2006.

University of Warwick. "Middle-Aged Misery Spans the Globe." *Science Daily,* January 30, 2008. Accessed September 14, 2019. http://www.sciencedaily.com/re leases/2008/01/08129080710.htm.

Vaillant, George E. *Aging Well.* New York: Little, Brown, and Company, 2002.

Van, Marilyn R. "The 15 Most Common Health Concerns for Seniors." Accessed March 12, 2020. https://www.everydayhealth.com/news/most-common-health-concerns-seniors/.

Volandes, Angelo E. *The Conversation: A Revolutionary Plan for End-of-Life Care.* Waterville, ME: Thorndike Press, a part of Gale, Cengage Learning, 2015. Large print edition.

Weiss, Matthew Cole. "20 People Who Did Great Things after 50." Accessed March 27, 2020. https://www.ranker.com/list/accomplishments-after-50/matthewcolew eiss.

Wengert, Timothy J. "By the Light of Grace: How Does the ELCA Understand Heaven and Hell?" *Living Lutheran* 3, no. 7 (October 2018).

Westerhoff, John. *Will Our Children Have Faith?* New York: The Seabury Press, 1976.

Williams, Mel. "Singing Our Way to Hope." Accessed November 15, 2019. https://fa ithandleadership.com/mel-williams-singing-our-way-hope.

Willimon, Will. *Aging: Growing Old in Church.* Grand Rapids: Baker Academic, 2020.

Wimberly, Anne Streaty (ed.). *Honoring African American Elders: A Ministry in the Soul Community.* San Francisco: Jossey and Bass, 1997.

Worden, J. William. *Grief Counseling and Grief Therapy: A Handbook for the Mental Health Practitioner.* New York: Springer Pub, 1991, 2002.

Yarnal, Careen and Xinyi Qian. "Older-Adult Playfulness: An Innovative Construct and Measurement for Healthy Aging Research." *American Journal of Play* 4, no. 1 (Summer 2011): 52–79.

Ziettlow, Amy. "Journeys of Care: The Roller Coaster, the Marathon, and the Deep End." *Christian Century,* September 11, 2019.

# Index

# Index of Scripture Passages